THOUGHTS *of a* A CONVICTED FELON
LIVE FROM THE L.A. COUNTY JAIL

CLINZELL "BOSS SPADE" WASHINGTON III

Copyright © 2021 by Clinzell "Boss Spade" Washington III
Los Angeles, California
All rights reserved.
Printed and Bound in the United States of America

Published and Distributed By
La Coasta Nostra LLC
Los Angeles, California
Email: lacostanostra0314@gmail.com
http://lacoastanostra314gmail.wordpress.com
Instagram: La_coasta_nostra

Packaging/Consulting
Professional Publishing House
1425 W. Manchester Ave. Ste B
Los Angeles, California 90047
323-750-3592
Email: professionalpublishinghouse@yahoo.com
www.Professionalpublishinghouse.com

Cover design: TWA Solutions.com
First printing October 2021
978-17377201-0-2
10987654321

No part of this book may be reproduced, stored in a retrieval system or transmitted in any form or by any means without the prior written permission of the publisher—except by a reviewer who may quote brief passages in a review to be printed in a newspaper, magazine or journal. For inquiry contact the publisher: zellionareblacc@gmail.com

In loving memory of my grandmother, Marva Elaine Hemmings, and my cousin, Douglas Earl Jefferson, Jr.

TABLE OF CONTENTS

PRODUCT OF MY ENVIRONMENT

Game Changer 11
Street Life 13
Loose Lips 15
Frienemies 1 17
Frienemies 2 19
Hate Rooted 20
Adrenalin Rush 21
Bump in the Night 22
Str-8 Hustin 23
Trust Issues 24
Save Our Youth 25
Trump Tight 26
Smile Now Die Later 27
Human City Dump 28
Hood Niggas Dream 1 30
Hood Niggas Dream 2 31
Snitch Factor 32
Speaking on Me, To She 34
Procurer 36
Gentrification 38
No Justice, No Peace 40

CELL TIME

Secret Admirer 43
Fight of My Life 44
Hate Me Now 45
One More Chance 47
Prison Bleu'z 48
Court Tanks 49
Game Over 51
County Jail Bleu'z 52
Con-crete Jungle 53
Replacing 54
Thinking About Her 55

Tomorrow is a New Day 56
Jail Bars and Karma 57

LOVE LETTERS

Prayer Going Up 63
No Words 65
Loyalty is Royalty 66
The Soloist 68
Girl from the Hood 69
Public/Closets 70
Whoever Knew 72
Crazy Bitch 73
Lost and Found 75
A Teenage Love 76
Side Chick 78
Crazy-ass Bitch 79
Do She Really Love Me? 81
Tangled Feelings 82

UNIVERSAL THOUGHTS

Life Swap 85
If You Be Mine (Aventador) 86
Everywhere 88
If I Could Fly 90
Astronomical Thoughts 91
For Better or Worse 92
Our World 93
Fear of Thee (Unknown) 94
Feel the Vibrations 103
Rise 104
Spread My Wings 105
Just Thinking 106
True Worth 108
Man's Best Friend 109

SPADE VS. ZELL

Real Talk 113
Welcome to My World 114
Lose, Lose Nation 119
Prisoner of My Thoughts 120
My Own Worst Enemy 121
Zell of the Jungle 123
Night-mariKKKa 125
Better Dayz 126
Me Against the World 129
AmeriKKKa Hate U.S. 130
Self-Destruction 133
Reflection 136
Bullets Don't Have No Names 137
Pillow Talk 139
9-2-5 140

IN THE DARK

Let's Take a Stand 143
Overcoming the Illusion 146
History of Shadows 148
Stars, Quasars, Pills and Portions 152
Sweet Land of Misery 156
The Trap 159
The Beginning of the End 160

OUR STORY VS. HIS-STORY

Colored Regiments 165
Eclipse of Wealth 168
Abolitionist 172
Treasure, Genocide and Slavery in Haiti 178
The Last Discoverer 181
California Queen 185
Stolen Legacy 187
Free Bodies of Lost Tribes 188
Crosses 189
Born and Raised in Captivity 192

Greenwood Massacre 194
El Yanga 196
Fight for Power 199
Black Caesar 201
Aztec Revolution 205
Aztec Evolution.. 206
Mercy of Ba'al 208
Stone Heads 217
King of Songhai 219

PRODUCT OF MY ENVIRONMENT

Game Changer

Just because we're both C.R.I.PS.
Doesn't mean that I need your help.
I'm a California revolutionary independent proud soldier.
Where is do4self.
I got money on my mind.
So I'm busy building on my wealth.
On another level now.
So the way I move is stealth.
Sneaky snitches be suspicious.
But I ain't doing no tellin'.
"Shit Nigga I'm Tryna Come Home (S.N.I.T.C.H.)"
Is what the fuck they be yellin'.
So I keep my ears to the streets.
Ride solo and stay with the heat.
Inside the LA county jail cells.
Niggas don't condone on those, whom prey on the weak.
While in the hood.
Bullies get fully'd.
For playing the act, of the big bad wolf.
But always watch out for the ones in sheep's clothing.
Yea! The one that you had to double look.
Can't even enjoy yourself at a hood day.
Because most of the homies are wolfs.
They said he died around all loved ones.
So how the fuck did all of his jewelry get took?
Niggas be pocket watchin'.
While waiting on that perfect hour.
Under the gloom of the Moon.
Is where his flesh was devoured.
By explosive blue tips and other cuz shot hollow's.
If the homies don't take you under.

Then watch out for the bitch around the way, with the hundred thousand follows and loves to swallow.
Any homies cum.
As long as he's getting that Guapo.
Bust them legs wide open and the pussy looks like a taco.
Can't understand what the hype is all about?
But over this one right here!!!
Big homie over there!!!
Will bust your head wide open, just like a nacho.
For money on the flow.
So many niggers will sell their souls.
How the fuck are you a pimp?
But never got no hoes?
How is homie still in the hood?
When he already told?
I guess the street game has transitioned.
Having a reversal of roles.
I wonder whatever happened, to all of those real-nigga sayings?
Like I'ma do it Foe Life!!!
Death Before Dishonor!!
And, Fa Death Doe!

Street Life

Shattered glass fragments, scattered abroad concrete.
Yellow tape surrounds a lost life, shell casing and tire streaks.
Anyone can get it.
"Bullets Don't Have No Names."
If you're in the street life, it's all a part of the game.
Funeral services, teardrops, Remy bottles and extended clips.
"Shorty Wanna Be A Thug."
Because his pops, was a real Crip.
But there's no future in jail bars, drug addictions and caskets.
Single parent homes in "Del Amo" are raising up "Bastards."
Carjacks, kidnaps and flocks turned into home invasions.
If you see sandals on the porch, the residence are Asian.
American flag poles, represent the home of a VET.
Surely you'll find a gun safe, full of ammunition, assault rifles, pistols and techs.
Or maybe you're a hustler ?
Because it runs through your veins.
Meth is on the rise, like in the 80s with crack cocaine.
Cartel wars are littering American soil with shell casings and bodies.
A prayer to Mal Verde will bring you wealth in abundance, Gucci suits, beautiful women and foreign coupes like Maseratis.
If it ain't worth dying for, then it can't be worth shit.
I know Killas doing life on the yard, who know the true meaning of worthless.
I'd rather hold court in the streets, than live out my days as a slave.
A prison cell forever.
Gotta to be worse than a grave.
If life is a gamble.
I guess my dice are loaded.
After I crack the game, pig out at a fine dine-in and sip champagne until my stomach is bloated.
Cliqoe, Ace of spades and Dom P.
Gone and order another round.

Because we got bottle service.
We keep secrets every Sunday.
Because I love the way she twerk it.
She's so high on that pole.
Baby looking like a fallen angel.
It's so much money on the floor.
That you can't even see her ankles.
Chocolate, caramel, olives and light skins.
Brazilian, Moorish, Puerto Rican and Mexicans.
I'm feeling like Willy Wonka, it's so many flavors.
Cuz got his nerves wifin' up strippers.
That niggas a hater.
Should have learned a lesson or two from Big Meech.
La Coasta Nostra is BMF without the drugs and we're less than 50 niggas deep.

Loose Lips

Our people are policing themselves, doing the job of the system.
Snitches are taking the stand and lying for compensation.
So please tell me, who's the real victims?
What started as a routine traffic stop, turn into a full-blown investigation.
Instagram and Facebook flicks, are obviously voluntary surveillance.
Hot spots, dope money, gang signs and guns.
Then came to search warrants and bailing out to run.
It's all fun and games, until somebody gets caught.
Now it's an Federal indictment and it's all your fault.
A sticky situation.
Catches a rat in the trap.
Your boy was wired for sound and now you're caught in the act.
Nowadays they snitch and then be right back on the block.
It's always the coldest killas.
You could believe me or not.
Those with hard heads, still associate with them.
Then when the cleaner shows up.
They both become his victims.
Life on the yard, ain't never been easy.
There's a shortage of real niggas.
Prisons are full of sensitive needings.
Your punk ass stitched and still got a life sentence.
While his crimey said he don't know shit and to the jury he was rather convincing.
Trying to get off easy, you told on somebody else.
But if you tell the whole story.
You'd have to implement yourself.
"Loose Lips."
Sink ships.
Don't end up like the Titanic.
Let your lawyer do all of the talking.
Because.
"You have the right, to remain silent."
So let's start taking advantage.

"Am I my brother's keeper?"
Everybody says yes.
But breed mixed with envy, made you shoot him dead in his chest.
If you'd kill your best friend, how could anyone trust you ?
The game don't love nobody.
So I stand on my own two.
If you want something done right, then you might as well do it yourself.
False moves by another.
Could just become compromising to one's wealth.
Always control the money and not ever let it gain mastery over you.
The only people with a price, are sell outs and prostitutes.
Real men stand tall and make their words law.
Firm standards to live by, with the posture of a boss.
Attitude reflects character and time unravels the truth.
If you're living a lie.
The world shall surely discover, the real you.

Frienemies (one)

Living in a future, where the past still haunts me.
Nothing close to a dope fiend.
But crime was my monkey.
I, grew up with some niggas, that I don't trust no-mo.
Crab's in a barrel, backstabbers and cutthroats.
Although he fed his team, his death was certainly suspicious.
Same dudes that wished he was dead, ended up being the only eyewitness.
So I keep my back to the wall, with my eyes to the crowd.
Finger on the trigger.
Man!!!
Them some phony-ass smiles.
Dagger's 4 pupils, slit like snakes.
A Sweet tooth Bates victims.
So, I baked them a cake.

In " The first 48," detectives be lurking.
No time to investigate.
When there's another three murkings.
The funeral was packed, even the killer made an appearance.
I could feel it in the air, it was all in-house dealings.
Blamed it on the rivals, then bury the burden.
Casualties come with war.
So, lock the doors and close the curtains.
History repeat itself and karma is thick.
How do the coldest Killers, turn out to snitch.
$50,000 to take the stand, is paid to snitches.
When niggas like that deserve, to be dead in ditches.
Tunnel visions of familiar faces, that's been planning my death.
While conversations with drug lords, are steadily building my wealth.
Never let the right hand, know what the left is up to.
Friend's turn into enemies.
Just like Bishop and Q.

Frienemies (Two)

The realest nigga that I know, is a credited to myself.
Same one you'd die for, will take your life.
Same mouth that said," I love you, my nigga!!! "
Is trying to fuck your wife.
The streets talk, so there are no secrets.
Put one ear to the pavement and you could hear "The Heart of The Streets" Beating.
You could follow the blood trail.
Because it's so many knives in my back.
Who needs enemies, when you have homies like that.
Elephant in the room and I could feel the radiance of your hatred.
No one recognized your walk, as to me there's a natural gravitation.
Friendly smiles and rough handshakes.
Are like the calm, before a storm, followed by an earthquake.
It's a thin line between Love and hate.
I tried lending you my hand and then got bit by a snake.
Can't give you the benefit any more, you've proved to be doubtful.
My clip is full of shells and you truly deserve a mouth full.
Only a coward thinks he'll live forever and creeps around as to avoid the fight.
Age will not spare his life, as he attempts to dodge these bullets tonight.
How foolish is he to believe, that all who smile in his face are friends.
He'll surely find out under pressure, when few are truly down for him.
Awake tossing and turning.
Sleeplessly worried about matters that he can't control.
Tired and stressed out by daybreak, as matter's still unfold.
I won't ever leave my heat, more than a step away when in these streets.
Constantly surrounded by foe's, Bros hoe's and frenemies.

Hate Rooted

Hate is an emotion, that reflects from self.
The man in the mirror and nobody else.
An inner wounded child, scarred deep to the core.
While skeletons in your closet, beat you down to the floor.
Laughing at the world.
But all along, the joke's on you.
You talk so much.
That you've unraveled the truth.
You're a wannabe.
Portraying to be.
What you'll never be.
More like the costume type.
Because your knife story is Halloween.
"Trick or treat, silly rabbit, Trix are for kids."
Hiding behind a mask, cocaine up your nose and a bottle of gin.
Talking Big Willie style.
But insecure are your thoughts.
Can't handle a real woman, so you often settle for thots.
Your conversation is below par, so social media is your savior.
Liking local hoe's pictures.
Captain cape crusader.
Throwing your dog's under the bus, in-boxing their bitch's.
No good game about yourself.
So you constantly be speaking on another nigga's business.
Telling your man's and 'em broad's.
The truth and nothing but.
How they be wife'n other bitches and treating some like sluts.

Adrenalin Rush

Nowhere to hide.
No one to trust.
One dead and two shot.
Just down the other block.
With only four shell's left in the gun.
As siren screams are getting louder.
I'm now on the run.
The powder bag was for sale.
But, in fear of apprehension.
Two lines I inhaled.
Now I'm feeling energetically uplifted.
As I took off my shirt to dust off, my pants and kicks.
Then of it and the weapon, were quickly dismissed.
Shirt to the left.
Burner way to the right.
Cut my pants into shorts.
Now, I have to avoid all of them red and blue lights.
Can't post at a bus stop.
Nor go to a burger stand and hide.
Gots to keep it moving.
Because, I'm still behind enemy lines.
Thinking to myself.
Just keep calm and stay focused.
But the reality of this whole situation feel so hopeless.
All of this.
Wasn't worth fuckin' a bitch.
In the wrong community.
Knee deep in some shit.
Draped in all blue.
With the tattoos of a Crip.

Bump In The Night

Clothing smelling of mildew, with holes in the soles of his shoes.
In the fall of night, he's the worst type of dude.
He doesn't hang out at liquor stores, with his hands out, carrying signs, nor begging for change.
More like sticking people up for money, car's, dope, iPhones and gold chains.
The reason women aren't safe, to walk through alley's.
It's all fair game to him.
Beatings, robbery, rape & stabbings.
No one is exempt from him stealing, everything that isn't glued to the ground.
Armed with a stolen revolver, from a detective's house.
A dog in the streets, in search of food.
Feeling kind of sick, he needed to shoot.
Up his veins and all through his bloodstream.
As the head nod's began.
For him, it was like living out a daydream.
Nowhere to run and not able to hide.
Tonight is the night, that his body and spirit devide.
Mumbling a quick prayer, to the most high of all.
He almost overdosed.
But, was saved by ice on his balls.
Barely escaping death you would think, a person would take heed.
This isn't his first.
But, more like third time this week.
It's just another day in the life, for the "bump in the night".
Now, it's time for him to load his syringe and take a long flight good night!!
Good night!!!
Goodnight…

Str-8 Hustlin'

Dope fiend, don't knock on this door no more.
But you could send your nephew over, if he's looking for scores.
I got that black, white, green, Molly and Roxy's.
All of my prices are fair enough, for all parties to eat.
Hard or soft, I got the zones for cheap.
Anywhere else in these streets, the going rate is 900 for bolders.
But with me it's 350 for the half and 200 for quaota's.
I'm the dopeman's, dopeman.
Whip it.
Then bring it back, A1 Yola.
If you need them chickens unplucked.
I'm gone call El Plaga.
He said it's kind of late, but you'll have it manana.
Plus you already know, that I got that super sticky.
But it's 28 grams and up, if you plan on fuckin' with me.
$400, 250 & that 175 shit.
Tweety five hundred dollars, thirty two and four racks a brick.
Anything in between, I'll surely make it fit the equation.
600 for an ounce of Molly, will have you feeling amazing.
But the M-30s are mainly, for my OT clientele.
I'm on that next level shit, weighing shit with no scale.
And, if my workers get caught up.
I'll hit my lawyer and by 12 they'll make bail.

Trust Issues

Same nigga's pattin' me on my back and dapping me up.

Would love to see a hole in my head, with my black Benz shot the fuc up.

But my higher power saved my soul, by locking me down.

Giving me a chance to better evaluate, situations dealing with full circles of clowns.

There were snakes in my garden, participating and treason.

Grilled garden snake salad, Oh! What a wonderful dish.

Decapitation before they even, get a chance to hiss.

These niggas ain't loyal and they love to travel in packs.

Trust will get your throat slit, or even stabbed in the back.

So I show No Love in the streets.

I'm more of a soloist, so I'll stay with the heat.

Keep my business dealings smooth and money stacked real neat.

I'm into finer things and your slitherously cheap.

Old heads are preaching a lost message.

And, can't stand my presence.

Maybe, because I am the future.

Rich homie like Quan and most of my haters are losers.

Save Our Youth

It's the events in our lives, that make us who we are.

But the choices that we make, defines whom we become.

In different case scenarios, some are worse than others.

Through a similarity of events, some become close like brothers.

The absence of a girl's father, could lead her heart to all the wrong places.

A mother's missing affection, could lead a son to expressing upon women disgraces.

When darkness show's up, it could be destroyed by light.

Your past, is the past.

And, a future could still be so bright.

It's not the teachings, but what's done by lessons learned.

When you work hard, you'll receive what's truly deserved.

Like making better days to come, by investing in our Youth.

What's best for them, should also be for you.

Let's focus more on the construction of our own family teams.

Leading by example in the community and supporting our local youth's dreams.

I've met mothers, that are jealous of their own daughters.

Gang members in prison, cell mates with their father's.

It's time to forever end, this continuous destructive cycle.

Shut down these revolving doors and together "Heal the World" like Michael.

Trump Tight

Uh! Uh!! Umm!!!
My throat itch.
Pimpin' shouldn't ever have to raise his voice upon a bitch.
This is a team sport and you need to play your position.
I'm a franchise owner in the game, still driven by my own ambitions.
But, before any more conversation.
You need to pay homage to these pockets by droppin them dues first.
Get rid of them renegade heel's and fill up this new purse.
I could see it in your eyes, a real spark of potential.
You need to live this Maybach life and get the fuck out them rentals.
I produce magic effects, by supernatural means.
It's only a tricks concern, if there's any more room In those jeans.
Turning of lost hoe's, into boss hoe's is the motto.
Put the pedal to the metal and banging gears full throttle.
As my tires turn, just like the wheels of fortune.
I'm shining bright like the sun and the summer is scorchin'.
I could be seen from a whole other Galaxy.
Diamonds around my neck, like a jewelry gallery.
Chilling wit' Pimpin' Rozay, on our Vamp Life tip.
I never get no sleep, because I be Pimpin' all night on a bitch.
By the end of the a.m. shift, my trap betta be Tight.
My bottom hoe piece, is a nigga that I use to know ex-wife.
No cane in my hand, because I don't walk with a limp.
Real players in the game, keep they game right.
While Pimpin' stay one up on a hoe and keep it "Trump Tight ".

Smile Now/Die Later
(Counterfeit Transactions)

Crocodile driving loafers on his feet, but the Breitling timepiece is all that you could see.
From the outside, looking into his Bentley GT.
Gucci shades hide the redness in his eyes.
Even the youngest of children, recognize he's no ordinary guy.
Kush smoke slithers through the sunroof like dancing snakes.
Combined with Kenny G jazz tunes, to mellow his wait.
Sitting in a daze.
Reflecting upon his younger days.
Growing up in the ruff and had to be tough.
Life lessons learned a long time ago, having heart just wasn't enough.
Money brings power and an iron fist demands respect in the streets.
Before he recognized it, he was in too deep.
Twice faint taps on the passenger window, brung him back to reality.
Of today's morality.
Before pressing unlock.
Glances were given to all mirrors, as he adjusted his Glock.
As the short Mexican entered and sat on the seat.
Almost, immediately they both gave a quick nod and shake as a greet.
Off they drove two lefts & a Swift right.
The migo directed him down an alleyway dark as night.
Half a million in Cold hard Cash counterfeit.
In exchange for a total of 20 kilograms, 40% Caine 60% bullshit.
Neither party had bothered to give a real check nor count.
Nods were exchanged again, this time no handshakes and both were so eager to bounce.
Both men parted with smiles on their faces.
But, eventually ended up dead in two different places.
All money, is not good money…
And the same thing that will make you laugh…
Could, also make you die such a beautiful death…

Human City Dump

There's a section in my city for lost souls, that will have one living in The matrix.
Not too far from the wholesale garment district.
24/7 anyone can score a fix of cocaine-heroin-pills-weed or you could even purchase a bitch.
Some go there to live comfortable as the opposite sex.
Hiding from their families and friends criticism.
But most overall to feed their addictions.
Drug dealers for business and others running from inner-city neighborhoods because of them snitching.
Rich white kids even pull up here, to score their dope.
Most of the time hustlers serve people, that they don't even know.
Crackheads comb through the streets, like schools of fish.
Some call it the bottoms, but I call it deep cities abyss.
It's enough money to go around, every gritter could get rich.
If it wasn't for the cameras and police everywhere that you look.

Plus, informants are on the prowl, because 10 years got them shook.
Some are so bold as to serve, right across the street from the precinct.
I've even seen smokers taking a hit, right in front of the door.
And two blocks down the police fuckin' a whore.
A homeless lady died last night under the bridge and the coroner discovered a quarter mil stitch in side of her jacket.
Dude used to be a millionaire, now he's a crackhead faggot.
A user jumped out of the fourteenth floor window, experiencing the most ultimate high.
Must have been listening to R. Kelly and believed that he could fly.
Same night that a white couple had been found dead in a car.
Syringes full of dope in both of their arms.
Federal agents watching everything unfold.
From high-rise buildings drinking coffee and eating donut holes.
If you come in from out of town and you need some advice.
Blacks got the small packs if you're a user.
But, if you're eating off a bigger plate holla at the Cubans.
East of Broadway from first to sixth.
The bottom of the bottoms deep city abyss.
Welcome to the human city dump, str-8 skid row shit.

H.N.D.

Hood Nigga's Dream

Every hood niggas dream, I want millions…
Money stacked so tall in boxes, scraping the ceiling…
I want a Maybach Benz.
So that I could recline in the back seat while I count my endz.
They told me money is evil, but it also makes the world go round…
And if I count 100 stacks, I'd bet your girl go down.
Because, she not thinking 'bout marriage with the horse and carriage.
Baby digging' on my jewelry and all of them karats.
She's acting like a bunny, but I treat her like rat.
Steady sniffin' for the cheese, because she heard I got stacks.
House in the hills, living large and in charge like Tony Montana.
Never smoking wraps, because we rollin' Grabba's fat like Chikita bananas.
Medical prescription for that orange, purple & blue.
I have to cop a quarter pound, of that sticky juicy fruit.
Whenever I pull up in the hood, all of my young soul-jahs salute.
But, some niggas on the sideline will still envy my steelo.
So, just in case a bitch nigga trip.
I keep a tight grip on this Desert Eagle.
And even though I'm papered up, I'm still livin' so illegal.

H.N.D.
Hood Nigga's Dream 2

Mo' money than you ever seen befo'.
Paper cuts on my thumb, so I bought a machine to count the dough.
But, you already know what it is my nigg…
The mo' money that you make, the more problems you get.
I'd rather be dealing with millionaire situations.
Instead of being bothered, with your average trials and tribulations.
Blessed in the game, so blessed all of my niggas with sacks.
Pounds of cocaine, got everybody counting racks.
No More drama, like Mary J once said.
Royal blue Maserati, but the Ferrari is red.
My garage is looking, I like a showroom floor.
Not to mention that the bar in my house, is looking like a liquor Bank store.
I can't trust my childhood friends…
So, I got AK's & surveillance for all of my uninvited.
In the flesh.
Boss status like Sosa.
True to life Self Made nigga.
La CoastaNoastra.
Guard dog's stomping the yard on patrol.
Like killer's with no parole, ready to insight a riot.

Snitch Factor

Where I'm from, my homies don't love each other
They'd rather see the down fall of
Someone he once called his brother
Old heads on the block, love to hate on the up and coming
Shootouts over cookie crumbs, and hood rats gone take the whole hood under.
The pigs will clean up the rest of the shit, with
Their shovels and rakes
Same niggas you grew up with are now working along with the jakes
They will snitch on you to the feds to
Get out some shit
Then once you're out the way
Gossip to your women about a whole other bitch
Fuck niggas be hella weak
And should have been born deceased
Too busy trying to destroy the welfare of somebody else
All due to you not being able to
Find a peace of mind to love oneself
You hatin' ass niggas
Never will win
I'm steady playin' in the field on
The all-star line-up and you
Steady ridin' the bench
I'm like Santa Clause when it comes
to gifts
Felix Mitchell passing out turkeys and
You're "pookie" slappin'
Yo smoker bitch
While I'm eating real good, you's a
Busboy
So when I'm done gone and wash
My dish

Thoughts of a Convicted Felon

I'm pretty sure by now, when you looking
In the mirror
You could recognize that you're truly a bitch
Snitching on close friends and distant
Family members
Just to get rich

SPEAKING ON ME, TO SHE

When you have friends like the
Ones I've got
Who needs enemies?
They truly are my frenemies
Same niggas I showed love
Put b4 my women,
Gave gratuity, words of encouragement
And friendly advice
Pillow talking to these hoe's
And everything got back to me,
That was said that night
I hope your conversation with
That bitch, was well worth it
She was quick to tell me all
You said and even how you
Were perkin
But I shut her down real quick
Because me no wit' dat "he say"
"she say" bullshit
But, don't worry my friend
I didn't give yo' bitch shit
Except fresh flesh to the lips
Before I bent her over for a few
Strokes and pounds to the hips
I don't have to say I'm a boss,…
Because, she could already tell
How much you speak on me
To she
Give these hoe's conformation, you see
Your bitch, see's right though you overstanding
That I'm everything
That you never will be
And it's no secret
I'm everything in a man she wants

Thoughts of a Convicted Felon

Your bitch see's right through you,
And it's no secret
At least according to all of the hood gossip, and
Loquacious leakage
I'm everything in the man, that she
Wants you to be
But, what she don't understand
Is that she will never be the one, to
The like of my degree
For the simple fact of fuckin with a
Nigga like you
Shows me all that
Needs be, for me to see
Because, you a dirty dick nigga who
Barely shower
Nor brush his teeth
You the type of nigga to fuck it
Up for your ex-bitch and
Have her quickly dismissed
Speaking on another nigga to a bitch
Is like a bitch
Fuckin a bitch
And if I wanted your bitch
I wouldn't ever get the pussy by
Speaking on you
Because bringing up your name
Would be the last thing, that I
Would do
As a matter of a fact
You should be mad at yourself
Because you gave the pussy curiosity
By speaking on me, to she

Procurer

Might seem kind of tall, standing on
The shoulder of giants
From a helicopters view, you could say
He's the flyest
Roll Royce phantom coming down
The street, without the opera
A smooth operator and very professional,
Just like a doctor
Not into selling dreams, but his life
Is a movie
No time for reading scripts, like
Austin Power he's groovy
A cowboy in gators, controlling
His women like cattle
Pimp'n is really going hard from
Atlanta, all the way to Seattle
He not doing no poppin' collars
Today, because he's got a
V-neck on
California weather is hot
So, these hoes working in heels
Wearing costumes and thongs
Shinning bright like the Northern Star
Rose gold between his lips and on
The wrist that Breitling
No black bitches allowed
Because they be out of pocket
Known for running hoe's off and willing
To slit a hoe throat to become
That wifey
That's why it's all snow bunnies, Asians
And Hispanics in his stable

He always had much love for his sistas,
But not if them hoe's ain't able
This is a lifestyle, industry, business
And a sport
Cracked a Puerto Rican hoe on Instagram and now she's on her way
From New York
Choosing fee is a G, but she
Brining me three
Love is pain, and the game don't
Love nobody

GENTRIFICATION

LEFT!! FACE!!
HALF LEFT FACE!! ATTENTION!!
PARADE REST!!!

Now stand at ease my nigga, it's a war going on and you may not even be paying attention.
This thing called re-gentrification will make you think twice about knowing.
Better than banging on a corner, that you prolyl never end up owning and its happening with alacrity, really approaching at a face pace you know????
They started off downtown, now they want everything in-between all the way to 102nd and Towne.
Down the street from the project, too!! Yeah!!! I'm talking right there in Watts.

2 bedroom loft homes will be built, and sold at a million dollars a pop.
Now just stop to think...whom will buy these homes??
I'm pretty sure before there even built, they'll already be owned.
Could yo momma afford that?? Or your rich dope dealing uncle even???
If so...I'm pretty sure they'd much rather spend they're bucks on a Moreno Valley-Lancaster or Victor Ville like the Jones, Hamilton's and Stevens.
First most of the Moors sold there homes to neighbors from across the border.
Now the whites want it all back, and are coming in enforcing their order.
And the rent you could expect to be going up for sure
It's called out with the old, and in with the newer.
They said it's time to destroy and rebuild.
The uprising of double story homes with swimming pools and long gated driveways.
Only a few short months after demolition.
He now wants to live right next to all that he hoards.
Who you think all of the building face lifts, new bike lanes, street signs, and true service of the laws are for?
Now you see them walking dogs in the evening, and in the morning driving their kids to school.
All they have to do is raise the rent, to get rid of most of the fools.
Everyone is running off towards the big houses, that are sold for the little bucks.
I guess that would be cool!! If we liked everything spaced out and far away from us.
Hot-dry-desert air, and instead of stray dogs, coyotes everywhere.
or maybe you're gonna shake the state, and move to Las Vegas, Colorado or Arizona.
Prolyl just move with relatives down south, and leave your brother in L.A. shooting dope on a corner.
It's not just happening in my city, this shits BIG I'm talking COAST 2 COAST.
And guess who are the biggest losers in this whole situation called re-gentrification?
SHII!IET you should already know!!!

No Justice, No Peace

From the North-East-West-South (NEWS).
What is our government going to do now?
I know.
Throw a few chump change dollars, at a few families. Then turn their backs on U.S. again.
If we don't fight back?
Please tell me.
How the fuck do we win?
First in 2012.
It was neighborhood watch men.
Killing unarmed citizens.
Then in 14.
Officers Nationwide, are on a murderous spree.
No one is safe.
Whom is going to police the pigs, that police me?
Or can we trust them either?
When they all have trigger fingers, that just seems so eager.

CELL TIME

Secret Admirer

Every time the wind blows.

I could feel your every thought.

Whispers say you're lonely as me.

Whether you admit it or not.

Your profession and my punishment.

Has brought our worlds to collide.

We find one another attractive.

The eyes never lie.

I could see us together as a couple.

You remind me of my ex.

And, maybe if I play my cards right.

You'll end up being my next.

Fight of My Life

As my thoughts drift behind these prison bars and concrete cell block buildings.
All I could think about is home sweet-home, family members, ex-lovers and all my children.
I can't believe that Klinya is already 10.
Carter is nearly half of that and Caleb is only two years behind him.
Time is of the essence and these years be flying fast.
But today is a new day and we could only live in the present.
While letting the past, be the past.
With that being said, there's always room to reminisce.
Although I've missed plenty of precious moments, new one's shall always exist.
I could have been home last October.
As we know that some thing's, are beyond my power.
But, please do believe.
When that day came, it was one of my darkest hours.
No deed goes unpunished.
As sure as there's nothing new under the sun.
As history repeats itself.
In one hundred and eighty days, I'll be paroling back to square one.
Perfect attendance at the " School of hard knocks."
So the knowledge, I've obtained is priceless.
Tryna stretch between a rock and a hard place.
Has me feeling, somewhat fight-less.
But I refuse to give up, right in the middle of the fight of my life.
As I bounced off of the ropes with an uppercut.
Jab to his chest and then knock him out with the right.

Hate Me Now

How could you possibly hate me?
When we've never even met?
No hi's.
Nor good-byes.
Not even a brief interact.
Here and now.
Is our first sight, of eye contact.
So, should I go off of your vibes and just hate you back?
Or, should I kill you off with this entity?
Of a more powerful energy called love.
Walked right up to you and just give you a hug.
Then could you possibly, still continue on to be so evil?
As to also hate me for that?
Or, maybe I should fuck your daughter?
Making her just another statistic.
Of another snow bunnies, heart being snatched by Mac.
Then, will that add more fuel to the fire?
Interbreed, with your darling baby.
Planting dark seeds, into your Creed.
Born to us will be a mixed daughter and her name shall be "Racey."
Through the deed of wanting to avenge, my ancestral of people's.
From this child we shall endure a portion of their wealth and land's in this sequel.
Inheritance, through marriage.
Taking your daughter's hand, under God's will.
Only for good head, sex and wealth.
She has a 3 million dollar policy.
So, there's no need to worry about her health.
Same as Europeans have, all throughout his-story.
Raped, dethroned and pillaged our stories.
Future, past and present.
Unbeknownst, to most.

We are all of a historical, Oracle of an energetic ball of wisdom's.
That's more mystical, then mysteries of the pyramids.
" I am, who I am," makes me whole.
Purity, is my soul.
Earth and I feed, on the same fruits of energy.
With the source, " I am one."
All things living, are part of this magnificent energy.
Including the universe, that surrounds our sun.
" Hate Me Now."

One More Chance

Trapped behind bars, has me lost in my thoughts.
I've tried the love thing before.
But, I guess she had a change of heart.
Feeling like I can't trust nobody.
Because, this world is cold.
Wishing I only had someone, that would console and soothe my soul.
Money is only paper, it can't ease this pain.
I need a real woman in my life.
Because, I'm done with all them games.
An angel walked out of heaven and visited me.
With the key to all my problems, seeming to set me free.
One thing I've learned here on Earth, is that promises are meant to be broken.
A past full of heartbreaks, had already left me feeling hopeless.
I deserve better than a woman, who could be so heartless.
Pain comes in many different forms of life and we all pay the piper regardless.
A feeling of knowing better, I'ma try it again.
Having nothing to lose, every game as a win.
It won't be so easy, she'll have to prove her heart.
Present joy to my days and bring me out of this dark.

Prison Bleu'z

Lonesome nights under the streetlights, are way different than lonely nights in a cell.
25 to Life on a prison yard, has to be similar to burning in hell.
No one likes to say goodbye, especially if be it forever.
There is no fairness in the "jew-dicial" system, in this corporation called AmeriKKKa.
3 strikes on a baseball field, are nothing like the one's in court.
You could lose your life by the fate of 12 strangers, without a second doubt, nor bit of remorse.
The other is controlled, by an umpire and it's only a sport.
Gang violence on the streets, while race riots spill blood in prison.
Rivals from different hoods, now are part of the same dominion's.
Correctional Officers encourage all racial segregation, in order to keep the bullshit going.
But, then they want to trip when they lose one of their own in this Omen.
Like that time in Chino.
A "C.O."
Passed a street knife to another race although
With the intent of a payoff, for making a Coast Crip member bleed.
Instead it was intercepted and the homie brought that same "C.O." down to his knees.
As he begged for his life, he was poked with 190 hole's.
Shortly after going limp, the homie Crip walk over his soul.
A life sentence.
He had already been sentenced.
A Blue flag tattooed across his forehead and being HIV positive was old news to him.
Talkin' about having nothing to lose.
This is a true story, on a matter that I've experienced personally.
While doing time with the homies.
In our "Prison Bleu'z"!!!

Court Tanks

If these walls could talk, everyone probably would end up with life sentences.
Niggas be so quick to tell their own and the next man's business.
When the paperwork came.
With recorded phone conversations, under your name.
Now, who's really doing the snitchin'?
Yo' homies tried to tell you, but you just wouldn't listen.
I swear some of you need to read a book for once.
Maybe, that'll possibly give y'all safer topics to discuss.
Like, next time think about paying a retainer for a lawyer.
Instead, of trickin' every night at the club.
Because, now your life is in the hands of a PD, making deals behind your back, with the da and a judge.
Now, you up in here hoping for fire camp and the life of a Sawyer.

Fat chance, if you keep seeking free legal advice from that jailhouse lawyer.

Because, he'll fuck around be the one to show up at your next court appearance.

The whole time he slid up under you, to build your case and lighten his sentence.

It's your own fault you're the one whom told him your whole case detail for detail all of the in's and out's.

Now, they got you by the balls way beyond reasonable doubt.

Got yo' ass ready to jump on the quickest deal.

Or if you're just another weak nigga, now you're ready to squeal.

I guess they say it ain't telling, when he was conversing with the detectives.

Because, the whole time that he was in there, he was only keeping it real.

GAME OVER

The game, is just not the same no more.
I think the snitch niggas done evened the score.
In California, they already took over the prisons indeed.
You could look it up online yourself, most of the yards are sensitive needs.
You better watch your front and the rear view.
Fuck being careful…
Don't say shit on them phones, because for sure they'll hear you.
Informants get audio recorders, installed in their stereo systems.
And, then they turn the beat down.
So, that the pigs could hear even the slightest whispers.
Every minute is a Kodak moment, due to the charms on their chains.
So, many pretend like they don't know who is doing the snitchin'.
Some hang to close and also end up drippin'.
Never trust a cat in the hood, whom talks too much.
Always the center of attention and running amok.
What, I tell you is true and purely all game.
And, if you get caught…
Never, speak your business inside of them tanks.

County Jail Bleu'z

I wonder if she could feel my pain.
I know I hurt her, but now I feel so lame.
The late nights out, not answering her calls.
Or sometimes, I wouldn't even come home at all.
Life in the fast Lane, fast women, fast cars.
Turning up late nights at bike club, strip clubs & in all of the inner city bars.
I was out chasing Molly.
Blaming all my problems on any and everybody.
But, in reality I have no one to blame for my mishap's.
Except myself and nobody else.
Now, I'm knee-deep in some shit and she still holding me down.
But, if I were out right now.
I probably be running around in another city wild or Maccin' another bitch down in a whole nother town.
Before, I got locked up crime was my everyday way of life.
Instead I should have been working on a legit career and making my woman my wife.
Ain't it funny now that I'm down, I think of this type of shit?
Tonight, I also wonder if she's getting fucked or sucking on another nigga's dick?
She put's money on the phone and answer's whenever I call.
But, women are way more slick than men, so I wouldn't doubt it at all.
I wonder if I knew, that for sure she was.
Would I give her room for error, or a chance to make a mistake.
I think as long as she continued to do for me, while I'm in here things will be okay.(Until I make it back her way.)
I'll be glad to see my lawyer walk into the courtroom and beat the DA down like it's Judgement Day.
Hopefully, I end up with a very lenient amount of time, my whole family would pray.

Con-Crete Jungle

There's no welcome mats in here, people are living in fear.
Flash light treatment stabbing slashes jackings and beatings.
White boys and Mexicans got love for one another.
But, yet and still…
Brothas can't find themselves to just simply love each other.
While race riots are poppin' off, some of the hardest niggas be running-hiding and acting soft.
Whomever is the last Man standing.
Deputies are tear gassing-shooting with block guns and are given flashlight to the Head bashings.
If you're Black you hope not to land on the wrong floor or dorm.
You're going to have to run some fades with rival gangs and you better perform.
But, if you happen to win too many fights.
You're so called own people are going to jump you, pack you out and try to put out your lights.

If you find yourself on the 2000 3000 or 4000 row.
You'll have a phone-bunk-toilet- three cellys-a set of jail bars-a ceiling-3 concrete walls and no windows.
You just got locked up a month ago, in late December.
Now you have to spend $10 for only an hour phone call, just to let your girl know that you'll be gone until November.
And, that's a light sentence.
I've been seeing them divide 1200 years between three people.
But, most end up getting a life sentence.
Domestic violence fight on your third strike, them pale-faces ain't playin'...
My nigga!!!
That's another life...
This is no place, for any human being.
So, it's best to bail out and then cash out on a real lawyer if you got that C.R.E.A.M.

Replacing

Red stars, blue hearts, purple kisses, yellow diamonds and candy coated raindrops.

Judging by this last rose petal, I guess she loves me not.

Just to think.

You're the one, I once thought I would die foe'.

Go to court and get acquitted.

'Cuz I'm the one, that you lied for.

It's been three and a half years now and the world as I once knew has gotten that much older.

Every winter, that passes me by.

I could feel your heart, getting that much colder.

That's around the time, when reality had set in.

I guess the words that I speak.

Versus theirs, is just of no comparison.

Collect call's, false rumors and conversations full of more allegations.

Now with only a hundred and eighty days left.

You've seem to have, suddenly

Run out of patience.

You expect me to cater to your every need.

All the while ignoring my ongoing trials and tribulations.

I need a vacation, some penetration and if you're tired of waitin'.

Then I guess you're the one, I'll be immediately "Replacing."

Thinking About Her

You remind me of a shooting star.

Because, you make me want to make a wish through your heart.

If I could, it would be.

That our love runs deeper than, the oceans abyss of dark.

If you were a ball player.

I'd be your number one router.

Having all of your collectibles from retirement, all the way down to when you first met recruiters.

All of the highlights of your career, would be memorialized and placed into frames.

Because it's obvious to me, that you're the best in the game.

L.O.L.

But, in reality you're way too short to be in the WNBA.

And, I don't think you could win in an Olympic relay.

Still and all no matter what my dear.

You will always be, my official rookie of the year.

You don't even have to be good at doing anything, other than being yourself.

Your love is so purely rich, that I could make it my very own wealth.

Tomorrow Is A New Day

Life is hard and love is pain.
When I mailed my heart out in a letter.
Her reply was.
Nigga please save that jail talk game.
When a nigga incarcerated, a bitch will talk to you any type of way.
But, their conversation change fast on that release date.
All the bullshit before, quickly comes to a cease.
I wonder by then…
Will we even be able to find time for Peace.
On the other side of these walls, the world is in full swing Coastin'.
On the inside and behind bars.
Everything seems to move, all in slow motion.
Every day is a repetition, like "Groundhog's Day".
For the past three months, she say's my words have been all the same.
Stuck between a rock and a hard place.
No windows in LA county jail cells.
Some mornings on the roof, is the only light of day.
1,000 push-ups, at 5 days a week.
Self-knowledge and education through my own personal readings.
Don't let the stress and long face fool you sweetie.
I'm gone touch down soon, steppin' in La Coasta Nostra shoes and having executive meetings.
Don't act like you don't already know, that I'm a boss.
Ever since that abortion, you seem somewhat lost.
I'm here for you baby and I've always been.
Don't get the acting up with the funnies now, that I'm on my way to the Pen.
Mined fucked up by this visiting window, instead of the tents of my Benz.

Jail Bars and Karma

Caged in a cell, just like an
Animal
If I were a beast, I'd prolly be
Like Hannibal
For these circumstances, I am
Not of the inhabitable
No money on my books, this week,
Eve must have run out of apples
All I can see are metal bars
Rats on concrete floors and roaches
On graffitied walls
Pigs patrolling in tan suits, with
Golden starts on their bellies
I can smell a fart in the air, from
One of my foul-ass cellys
He came in kicking heroine, just the
Other night
Woke up this morning in need, of

Something sweet to fix his appetite
So, I tossed him two fireballs, and
A pack of snicker doodles
Then bust down a bag of chips, to
Eat with my noodles
My bag of pruno, should be ready
Tonight
Hope I don't get too drunk, and
Get into a fight
Get to baggin' on a nigga, who
Can't take the pressure
Like I need some head right now
Your girl looks cool, but yo'
Mama is better
It's all in fun and games, until
Somebody gets hurt
Damn she thicks in that
Picture, is that yo' mamma
In a skirt
"LOL" my nigga
I'm just playin I'ma stop with
The mamma jokes
I needed them laughs, but its time
To call my bitch on the phone
She excepted the call
Hello!!! Ummm!!!
W.T.F,!!! Dis this bitch just moan !!

LOVE LETTERS

Prayers Going Up

R.I.P. Samantha Clarice Sherman. I love you, girl.
I remember it like yesterday when you first walked into my world.

We both were teenagers,
but you were just a few years older than me.

While I was attending Dodson Junior High,
you were in high school, going to Banning.

We met in a two-week, juvenile probation course;
all sentenced to do hours by the juvenile courts.

When I say all,
I mean that siblings were involved.

My brother, Kameron, got caught ditching and I did a burglary,
while Samantha, April, Lolly, and their younger brother, Paul,
all got caught stealing from the Del Amo Mall.

It all started with childish games and seductional flirts,
while everyone else was already fuckin'.

Hisa and Samantha were the oldest.
Both still virgins.

April and Khalani were two youths, really putting that work in.
That was way before scrapes, jerkin', and twerkin'.

Alicia was a little younger,
But still hung out sometimes.

Felicia was still a baby.
I think she was like five.

Goddamn.
Thinking and writing about this shit.
Got me feeling like an old man.

If I could remember it right;
I think this was around '96 or '97.
We all went to the movies and saw *Rush Hour* together.

Kameron, Chris, Lydale, Paul, Deon, Marcel,
Maurice, and the twins are my brothers forever.
A group of childhood friends that still call on each other.

Inside of the LA County jail is where I found out Samantha went under.

Me and Ali were cellys in the pen
when he told me all about how Marcel got murdered.

So, I wrote this in loving memory of my cousin Lil Marcel,
and one of my childhood lovers.

Rest in peace, Samantha.

We all know.
How much I loved her.

No Words

The look in her eyes.
Said, Paradise.
This couldn't be the first time.
We've had to have met twice.
Maybe we've engaged, in the another life.
A woman of such beauty and distinction.
I'd surely, could never forget.
I could feel an unseen force of energy.
The way she pressed it upon me so vibrantly.
Soulful body language.
I understand her clear, so very clear.
An addictive feeling that left me higher, than the stratosphere.
My heart rate must have sped up.
Because I could feel, it pulsating faster.
While me and the homies are chillin at the bar.
They're all having a good time smiling and going in on the liquor hard.
But, I'm so tuned into she.
That I can't even hear their laughter.
I like the way she move…
Sashaying around the dance floor, with the rhythmualism of her own so smooth.
A Kodak moment she is indeed.
As she takes selfie pics, they're more like captures.
All the while.
I'm so " Caught Up In The Rapture."

Loyalty Is Royalty

I'm just going to be honest from the start.
The way our conversation, on the phone had begun.
I'm not going to lie, it was hella slum.
Then by the end, when the line was hung.
I really feel like with it went, some air from my lungs.
It felt like you tossed a rock, through a stained glass window.
That was an exact replica of my heart.
My body was an abandoned building.
It felt, so real then.
Like a raw ass, very uncomfortable feeling.
I don't know if your anger was truly meant for me.
But, if it was?
Or not?
I'm going to need some healing, until this feeling stops.
The way you had, spoken to I.
Last night, just felt so foreign.
I said, I love you!!!
And, I couldn't get an I love you back.
If it's the truth that you think, I can't handle?
I'd rather find out here and now.
Rather than to later on here about the scandal.
I truly love you my sweet.
While also understanding.
That while I'm here in a cell.
You still have needs.
A horny red nose, running loose through the city.
Feeling like a bitch in heat.
But, if you feel like I'm not worth the wait?
Then, believe me when I say.
That we need more than just a break.
I'm more than willing.

To still dismiss women.
Here and now.
"Live from the LA county jail."
And, even from a prison cell.
So, I hope you don't feel exempt from that.
Because, I need a real woman behind me.
To stand tall.
Through it all.
And, really have my back.
I'd hope none of the strongness and support you would lack.
A true Queen in my life.
I'm a boss in this world.
Coming from a bloodline, of nothing but Kings.
So, in my life time setting.
I can't accept nothing, but respect from these niggas.
And, from my woman.
I deserve nothing but, pure loyalty from my queen

the soloist

Her walk is full of so much confidence.
She strides with pride, just like a black stallion.
I've never met a woman so proud, of the way she gets that dough.
A hundred, on top of hundreds!!!
A thousand, on top of thousands!!!
Colorful heels so bright and costumes that fit pretty tight.
A day off is unheard-of, she even works on Christmas night's.
She has the same resolution for New year's, every year!!!
That's to triple her trap, from all of the past years.
Time to relocate and change states, in order to get that money more faster.
A squares love is not for she and will surely leave he in disaster.
No sex without a condom.
But, first hand over the money.
She's a renegade, in a man's game.
Tearing it off or herself she say.
Because, her mama ain't raise no dummy.
Walking the blade like a tightrope, with precaution and persistence.
Pimpin' don't like fag hoe's.
That are aren't being instructed by "IZM".
In her craft of life, she considers herself professionalism.
Hard at work, so there's no time for buddy and up.
Fraternizing with lost hoe's.
Is the easiest way, to get caught the fuck up.

Girl From The Hood

In a zone high ass fuck on this mountaintop.

Picking rose's thinking to myself, she loves me! Oh shit she loves me not.

How could a woman so beautiful, be so ugly on the inside.

She probably is an inner child wounded on the inside!!

Maybe it was her upbringing or possibly past heartbreaks.

Now, playing for keeps at way bigger steaks.

She's passing that pussy around to whomever has the biggest cake.

She keeps her own condoms, because she ain't having no kids.

At the club every Thursday night, with all of the local hoods lusting over her head.

She has her own moves, she don't do the twerk.

The homies loves her, because she's a rider and down to put in that work.

The head topic of discussion, of niggas behind jail bars.

She don't have her own, but quick to pull up in one of her niggas' cars.

As I take a deep look into her eyes, I could see her soul cry.

I heard when she is alone, she wishes that she could die.

Been to prison before, but suicide is hard time.

I send my heart out to you, that you get your life together.

I just hope that you don't end up all alone, on the coldest winter ever.

Public/Closets

Born to Mack, meant to be like four doors on a Cadillac.
Mac a bad bitch from the US to the UN.
Two days later catch me ridin' in a new Benz. Not showing off for them, but just blowing in the wind.
Breaking hoes down to the very last compound like syllables.
It's only two types of freaks that I know.
Public freaks are the most easiest of targets.
She wears seduction, surely as a Dalmatian's coat is spotted.
For sex is a weapon-tool-trade-hobby and her job.
Catch this bitch hungry enough and pussy could be exchanged for a bite of shish kabob.
Not a five-star restaurant, nor four-course meal will be of the insists.
The bitch will simply settle for meat on a stick.
But, that's enough about her…
Now let's get on to this closet bitch.
In comparison to a ninja in a tree, or thief in the night.
She likes to keep it on the low, but most definitely will satisfy your

appetite.
All around the world it's the same old song.
School teachers, nurses, bus drivers and police women all wearing their thongs.
Like, Love, Lust or just fun fucks makes no difference to her.
As long as things are kept discreet and quiet as a cat's purrr…
At first sight or invite she will surely play the role as if she don't do.
But if you're a real nigga, you already know that ain't true.
But, sooner or later her inner animality instincts will come out one night.
Like, a Florida Gator she could devour you whole in just one bite.
To the one who didn't know (squares), what type of bitch he'd be dealing with.
May be left shocked, sprung and dumbfounded…
With his left hand on his head and right on his hip.
Come to find out this bitch done turned tricks, can do the splits, love it in her ass and can suck one hell of a dick!!!

Whoever Knew

We've been through so much together.
We even survived the coldest winter ever.
You're my homeboy sister.
And I was your Mister.
It all happened so fast.
I even knew a few men from your past.
In both of our situations, we had to accept the good with the bad.
Indeed a very lovely woman you are.
Caught up in the rapture, you loved so hard.
When we made love, it was like we made music together.
& every time that you sucked my dick and swallow that shit.
I could remember thinking to myself, nobody does it Better.
Out of all of the women that I've ever been with.
You are surely one of the best.
If we had met on the dating game, I would have eliminated all of the rest.
I remember when the streets found out that you were my lady.
People who I thought I was cool with, immediately committed to hating.
I could tell the homegirls thought even less of you.
Under the bright rays of the Sun.
You even accepted my daughter and son.
Now that you have conceived.
It seems as if, you couldn't believe.
I'm sure Klinya & Carter will be happy about their younger sibling.
I loved you, because you were my love.
So once again.
I would like to thank you, for all the good you've done.

Crazy Bitch

I could tell this woman was used to the roughneck types.

I guess she thought that I was the same, because when we met I was with my crew that night.

Looking into the open window of her soul.

I could tell she was in need to be consoled.

Honesty, Love, Protection and Affection is all that she needed from me.

Born rich she had inherited millions in Belize at 3.

Her parents had passed in a fatal car crash.

So she never had a real father figure in her life.

To teach the truth values of how a man, should treat and love his wife.

Abuse, physical, mental and verbal is what she was used to in past relationships.

So my kindness, devotion and concerns she had been so quick to dismiss.

At first she would take my kindness for weakness.

Until she took the time out to understand, the lessons that I was teaching.

Thinking she could manipulate love, she tried to buy my heart.

Not even knowing I was born to Mac like Too $hort, & I was just playing my cards.

Shopping sprees jewelry pieces and fine dine in's.

Was not merely worth, how this relationship would end.

It all started with her closed fist and aiming at my head with objects.

I not never once time responded back with violence.

Instead I would restrain and refrain while yelling at the top of my lungs.

"You better stop bitch!!! bKuz I am not the one!!!"

Things really went South, when I stopped giving her threats.

I showed her just as promised…

Yeah, I was most definitely done with her shit.

She started stalking my parents' house, along with every corner I hung.

Even made up a fictitious story, that had my PO on one!!

Once caught on a violation, I thought I was only running.

She told him that I carjacked her and it was a very brutal run-in.

Sooner than later I was cleared of all charges, like a sunny summer sky, on a unclouded day.

Now, every time that I see her, she still apologizes till this very day.

But, I only give her looks of discuss & dismay.

But, she gotta live with the fact, she has my name tattooed down her arm.

All I have from her are these distant memories & this muhfuckin' poem.

Lost & Found

The first time that our pupils met, it was such a vibrant thing.
I fell into an immediate trans of an awakened slumber, something like a sensual day dream.
She had the swagger of a cobra, swaying back and forth to the seductive tunes of a flute.
Olive green eyes, with the most amazing body.
Gucci pocketbook in hand, while the cashier was ringing up Jimmy Choo.
Two stores down, I continued to Coast.
Until she comes my way, I have found my post.
As I gaze at the shoppers just below and over the rail.
Brainstorming up a plan to seduce her well.
Oh shit! Here she comes and she's headed right at me!!!
"Excuse me Miss I'm sort of lost, could you please direct me?"
Her reply was…
"My apologies, but I'm not really a local"
Come to find out she was originally from the east coast and just recently became bicoastal.
"Luckily for you this is my city and I would love to show you around."
"In exchange for your company, I'd consider myself found."

A Teenage Love

I remember the first time, that we had laid eyes one another.
We both paused Doe-eyed, & I knew that someday she'd be my lover.
Although neither of us, had spoken one word to each other.
It was obvious, that she had wanted me.
Just as bad, as I had wanted she.
Surely, that next day curiosities were raised.
Our mutual party was hit with a thunder storm of questions, that excitedly came from both ways.
"Who is he??"
"Who is she???"
"She, said you're cute."
"I think she's fine!!"
I guess playing Matchmaker was fun for Lanae, and of course I didn't mind.
With all of the lust in the air, we'd quickly forgotten about the only problem.
She had an older boyfriend, but she surely would solve him.
By the next week's end, he was kicked to the curb.
Then we paraded through the streets, like two lovebirds.
She was fully developed as a teen and resembled LeToya Luckett in a group called Destiny's Child.
Everywhere that we went, I felt that I had the baddest around.
I could do nothing but give a proud grin and think to myself.
I'm so lucky and smile.
She was a virgin and I had only been with one other back then.
But, now she was ready…
Perfect timing because my aunt was going to Vegas and was going to be gone for the weekend.

Even though she was my second time around, it felt like it was both of our first.
Probably because I lost my virginity in a train, and the woman was the same age as my mother.
After that we continued to explore each other, as sexual lovers for the next few years.
Until one day this beautiful thing of ours, all ended in her tears.

Side Chick

Is it me? Or could it be she?
IDK?
But, it seems as if our relationship is constantly reminding me, of what everything is not supposed to be.
I got love for her...
When she's clearly in love with me.
But, my feelings don't run as deep.
For the chick who sucked my dick three times last week.
Her performance had no flaws.
So I took her to Benni Hanna's, in place of an round of applause.
We shared a few laughs, over appetizers and drinks...
But, I awoke next to my woman instead of she.
"Good Morning My Love!!!"
"How was your night??"
I made some breakfast, would you like to have a bite?
"Yes, Babe. Indeed that I would like, but first let's build up on a larger appetite!!!"
As I grabbed at her waistline, simultaneously engaging to fuck...
Her pussy is so good, and that ass is on buff.
That's when my phone starting blaring, with that one text tone...
Nothing, romantic.
But, more like a gangsta rap song.
When I finally got a chance.
This is what the text read...
"Good Morning!! My sis told me that she made you breakfast in bed."
"But, as soon as she leaves for work shoot me a text. & I'll swing by to give you some more of this head"

Crazy-ass Bitch

As I look at this photo of
You and me
I'm reminded of what our love, once used to be
I must have been misconstrued,
Thinking you were meant for me
Delusional in my thoughts, that we'd
One day start a family
If I were the man with the pants
I guess you wore the coveralls
A crazy-ass bitch, you were indeed
Overall
Every night you would fight, cuss, scream
and stagger in drunkenly
I'd just hop in the whip and sagg off
Comfortably
In my mind,
I knew that would hurt you more
Mentally
But being the crazy-ass bitch, that you are
You would anticipate physically
Phone calls and texts would come
In all night
No answers, nor replies and I'm pulling
Up at sunrise after 3 consecutive
Nights
Now that you're sober, you want
To apologize for being so trif
Claims of blackouts, bipolarness and
Being mentally unstable were the
Main cause of the fights
Come on now baby girl, you done said
This shit plenty of times before
So gone and put it all over there,

Right on that shelf
Because if it's a fight win a man
That you want
You could've gone and do that shit
With somebody else
I'd rather just kill you like O.J.
Before I put my hands on you
Any day
So I'm gone keep these cuff links
Cleans & my sleeves white
As a dove
It might sound a little fuck up,
But for real, I write this all out of love
You need to first seek some therapy
Before you continue seeking
For love

Do she really love me?

Do she really love me ?
How could I tell ?
Living a life of crime , would she stick with me through jail?
If I took a bullet to the head?
Or pushed her out of harm's way , and felt a bumper for her to prove my love…
Would she stick by my hospital bed , if I was in a coma for a year?
Not knowing if I'd survive or die??
Do she really love me?
If I fell down two flights of stairs
Got paralyzed and nobody else was there
What about if I'd got caught in a back draft rapture
Surviving with 3rd degree burns from there after
Do she really love me?
The way she constantly repeat it
The way she screams my name , when I'm all up in that pussy "beatin"
I wonder if I was hurting
And I were nowhere around
Something like miles away
Would my phone suddenly ring?
And then when I answer , will I hear her say
I was just callin because I really love you
And from here , I could feel your pain
Do she really love me?
That a question that deserves a real answer
If she asked me
I would say yes!!! To all the above
Even if she had , real bad cancer
She I would always love.

TANGLED FEELINGS

Love could be so blind, even with your eyes wide open. Relationships are built on trust without that they're nothing. I gave you all of me, in exchange for your heart.
I'm down on one knee a ready?
Or not?
Give me your hand and be my wife.
For better or worse, let's do it for life.
Joined together as one and form our union.
Start our own family.
Then annually have reunion's.
Be my empress and we shall reign supreme.
Every woman wants marriage, so let's live out your dreams. I promise to be the best.
Forever true to you.
Stay down for me and I always will be for you.
Is our love strong enough ?
To survive a prison bid ?
If I wife you up, will you accept my kids ?
Are you so vulnerable, as to give that pussy away ?
If you do ?
Will the way I love you stay ?
Accident's happens, what if you ended up pregnant ?
If you have another nigga's baby.
Truthfully, I would never accept it.
Then we will part ways and say bye forever.
I love you unconditionally.
So, I might cry forever.
Maybe, not boo-hoo.
But, tattoo my tears.
Rest in peace my love.
To our unborn child my dear.

UNIVERSAL THOUGHTS

Life Swap

Even the most experienced, well-traveled of a man.
Points of views can change, with the loss of one's plan.
From "King of the Hill," to a small fish in a big pond.
From the world at his feet, to holding out empty palms.
Suicide is a thought, easier said than done.
Millionaire on a prison block, or the life of a bum.
Now which of the two, would you say be of the preferred.
Giving my own opinion, they both seem absurd.
Forced standard living.
When you're clearly, accustomed to more.
Or limitless freedom.
But starving and sleeping on floors.
If given the opportunity, maybe they would trade place's.
Overcome the inevitable and learn from the others mistaking.
One man's trash, is another man's treasure.
If only life were so simple.
Do you think the world, would be better ?
The art of mindfulness and practice of outer body experience.
A conscious mind state, during the transfer of spirits.
But would that be enough ?
To satisfy, one's faults.
Or will they want more ?
In search of another life swap.
Greed is never full.
When it's appetite, still has an hunger for more.
Something like…
Robbing for millions of dollars and still out looking for scores.

If You Be Mine (Aventador)

I love everything about you.
Your body shape, foreign accent, open mind and the way you torque it.
All my ex-lovers will surely be jealous of you.
Our Bond is unconditional and although you came upon me platinum gray/silver.
I'm thinking about draping you down in all blue.
Every time I climb inside.
They be up in the sky and feels so good when they come down for the ride.
Your insides make me feel right at home.
If you promise to be mine, I will never leave you alone.
We can do this thing all night.
Then fall asleep with each other when the sunrise.
Or we could wait until the next moonlight.

At half a million.
You're way too expensive to be a hoe.
So all of the joy that you bring me, my haters will never know.
When kids see us together, they give me my props.
As I ride by waving my middle finger to the CHP.
Screamin' "Fuck the cops!"
If you be mine…
I will never give my heart to another.
All you have to do is say, "Yes!"
I'll be your lover.
" Secret Sunday " strippers, drop it pretty low to the floor.
But I haven't met one yet, that could get down lower than yours.
To prove my love I would like to make, " A Public Service Announcement."
I'm sorry Lexus and Porsche it's over…
Oh yeah!!!
Mercedes, I'm done with you too!!!
Lamborghini Aventador roadster.
I Will always Love you.
Picture me coastin'!
Draped in all blue.

EVERYWHERE

I can feel it in the air.
Especially in powerful wave's, high tides and mountain tops that flow with high intensity winds.
This elegant flow of purified energy is so amazing.
I feel as if I could do anything and it doesn't even amaze me.
Those unbeknownst to these feelings, are left in the awe of dark.
When all they have to do really, is open their heart.
Let natural currents flow and through your soul.
You never know what lies beneath to behold.
But first we must let go of all of the egotism and many other unhealthy substances that clog's the heart.
Reverse the bullshit.
Then come a new from the start.
Television, social acceptance, worries, rushing and hurries.
All of these things are stressful and unhealthy burdens.
Work on a better you, for better days and better ways.

Preparation, meditation, compassion, mindfulness, better eating habits, embracement of flaws and generosity.
Maybe even take time away from the cities high speed-fast paced energies.
Spend time with nature.
Feeling its full effects of spirituality, wholeness and embracefulness of another kind of synergy.
Become one.
With oneself.
Accomplish these practices and guaranteed one shall live in greater health.
Feel a new self-worth, in an abundance of inner wealth.
But first, you must take the time to think.
What are you worth to yourself?
Now, ask!!!
Do I really love myself?
It's time to destroy the nasty old habits and recognize the floss from within.
Work on the rebirth and reconstruction of thyselfs inner diamond cuts, rubies and gems.
One must help self, before one could call one's self helping another.
If you can't help yourself?
How are you going to help your sisters and brothers?
We could learn a lot from the Buddhist.
But I'm not saying go and become a monk.
What I'm saying is.
Like new keys, to new cars.
Let's open up, new trunks.

If I Could Fly

If I could fly.
I would spend a lot of time in the sky.
Not on no supernatural, unhappen-able, only imaginable type of thing.
Like the archangel, on the X-Men had his wing's.
What I'm saying, is exactly what I mean.
Like if I were a billionaire and I owned my own plane's.
I'd probably live in the air.
But, for sure me and my women would make love up there.
Every time, I'd take a flight.
I would pack blunts, rolled with flight.
Then I'm sure to experience the thrill, of the highest of all heights.
No one would be, higher than me.
Other than, Almighty Thee.
Greatest ever, to feel my energy.
Every time I'd look below, I wonder what I'd see.
But, one thing's for sure.
Is that, I would make plenty of stops.
Because living my life, all the way at the bottom.
Has me wanting to, feel the air up top.
No longer worried about cops and now living an ungoverned life.
I probably would become sovereign and in every continent.
I will have a different wife.

Astronomical Thoughts

Dreaming I fell off of the Earth, on some deep space shit.

Then got an orgasm, from a gravitational pull sucking my dick.

I penetrated "A-Star", thicker than Nicki Minaj.

Before I exited our solar system, I blew a blunt on Mars.

Got into my space Porsche, then headed to the 12th planet.

Hungry for a snack.

I made a stop along the way, at the milky way.

Dipped some Oreos and then was on my way.

The art of my astral aviation.

Was led by my great internal thoughts, of navigation.

When I had finally reach my destination.

It all seemed like this whole planet, was so eagerly awaiting.

For Better or Worse

Trapped in this maze of a Rubik's cube.
Chiseling at patterns, trying to make it through.
Green, yellow, red, white and blue.
It might take me a whole 3 years, to get back to you.
Just when I get to one solid formation.
I end up with more trials and tribulations.
My eyes are bucked, from demonic shadows on the wall.
Skeletons are chasing me around the room, from a past I caused.
A feeling of, feeling lost.
Has left me with no choice, but to find myself.
Feeling unloved.
I had to love thyself.
How could I have caused, myself so much pain.
Trying to conceal these tears, as I run through this rain.
Sometimes I feel as if, I'm my own worst enemy.
Had to get rid of self-hate and then in inveterate self-worth in me.
No longer do I feel like, I have nothing to lose.
With all of my worth, I want was owed and due.
Visited by an Oracle, in my dream.
That day I remember waking up feeling, so utterly supreme.
A bowl full of knowledge, is what I received.
That was just before, I was hailed to be king.
Dreams feel like movies.
While my reality feels more like, a chess game.
Trying to fight my way back home, to my queen.
By changing my strategies, I've changed my life.
I think I'm finally ready, to make her my wife.

Our World

Without you my love, there is no me.
You're the other half of my circle, we make us complete.
Without me, there could be no you.
Together we're like heaven and earth, latitude and longitude.
You are the heart, while I'm the beat.
Without one another, we'll end up deceased.
You're mother Earth and I love you're nature.
I'm every sea, ocean and Coast.
While the sky is our neighbor.
A world of love, peace and equality.
Earthquakes and hurricanes are no longer called natural disasters.
Instead they're ruptures of our orgasms, when we get a caught up in the rapture.
It usually starts off slow, before we get to going faster.
I left your shore wet, besides a few waves the ocean is now calm.
As your earth had finished pulsating, the world experienced an aftershock.
Then we accidentally destroyed, most of the boats along the docks.
But, now we could stop.
Because this was the end of round two.
After that.
We both fell asleep, while looking at the groom of the Moon.

Fear of Thee (Unknown)

A lot of people fear living life.
On regular terms, as the world turns.
Wishing that they could escape, looking up as a sunburn's.
Fear of their own reflection.
Because of the truth behind, the one in the mirror.
This plays a large factor in the life of a person, that has been resisting change out of fear.
For fear of the unknown.
Too afraid to grow up and live life grown.
Rather live the life, of a second childhood.
Couch potato way's, while playing video games in their parents' home.
Girlfriends can spend the night.
Every night.
Or even live rent-free under your armpits.
Just keep food in the fridge, clean up after the kids and make sure the chores are did.
The young bird.
Too afraid to leave the nest and find a home of his own.

Fear of Success

His mom put the rock in his hand, when he was only two years young.
She gave him the best of everything and of course a love unconditional.
He'd never, met his father.
So, he yearned for him additional.
Mom's kept fresh to death.
And, on the court he was surely one of the best.
But, due to being afraid of certain aspects in life.
He'd chosen self-destruction, instead of taking his flight.
The poor boy grew up, torturing himself.
Afraid of being the best, by living out his dreams.
In fear of success.
All throughout his days of school.
He'd had all of the finest of girlfriends and even the bully's thought he was cool.
Straight A student, class valedictorian, & Mr. popularity himself.
Crossovers and three pointers.
But, always been a team player to the rest.
Even took his school to the state Championship.
But, it was more than obvious to his mother.
That he blew, the game-winning point on purpose.
Too afraid to move on.
When most of his friends futures, seem to have no purpose.

Fear of Commitment

How could a woman be so heartless?
When he was in love, with she?
His heart more pure than gold and he was born in eternal.
As if erupted into a ball of flames and burning inferno.
The first love of his life.
Had cost him everlasting heartbreak.
Left him feeling used and embarrassed, like a one-night fling on spring break.
When his mother walked out of his childhood, she also stole his innocence.
Left her only son, afraid to Love.
Hard to get emotionally involved, living in fear of commitment.
Max Julien, Iceberg Slim, Too $hort&Pimpin' Ken.
Exposed me to different lifestyles, of how to be a pimp.
Love is four squares and being heartbroken was for simps.
Fast cars and fast broads.
Living life on a schedule, something like a movie star.
Club hopping on weekends.
From White bar's to Paisa bar's, collecting them ends.
Sliding down the track, in a brand new Benz.
Smooth sailing like a kite in the sky.
Just blowing in the wind.
And although there's profit in other people's pleasure.
A hoe's love.
Still will never be enough, to make him feel any better.

Fear of Disapproval

Born in Mexico.
But, Maria has been in the U.S. since three.
She'd even grew up in a barrio, not too far from me.
Under the roof, of her parents' home.
There was no such thing as free will.
Nor, freedom of speech.
Her father wore the pants and all her mother could do is agree.
Maria's entire childhood, was full of forced ideologies of hate.
Taught, trained and groomed.
To stay far away from their, darker-skinned neighbors.
That not only rape.
But, also kill, steal, rob, beat, stab us and burglarize our homes.
They're so such animals.
That they even do, these same sorts of things to their own.
Maria and her siblings knew to never, bring any friends home of the such.
Most certainly, under any circumstances.
No Men, of their bunch.
But, secretly she had a best friend named Tasha.
Eventually, Maria and her new friend's brother.
Marcus, whom was too years older.
Started hooking up on a regular and had become new age lover's.
By the last year high school, she clearly was showing.
Her father had disapproved.
Yelling at the top of his lungs, in Spanish racial slurs.
"My own fucking daughter!!! Is a real Niger lover!!!"
She was then kicked out of her parents' home.
Marcus, would never leave his child's mother in this cold world alone.
She'd always been accepted, by his mother.
So she was welcomed to stay with open arms and treated as one of their own.

Now, Maria's mother is the one sneaking around.

Buying gifts for and visiting her newly-born grandchild.
Meanwhile, her husband was still stuck in his ways.
Intolerant, skeptical, unsupportive and filled with rage.
A man of racist feeling's, that he always would hoard.
In which these are facts, that he always avoid.
Although he would never admit it, he knew it was his own fault.
That things had happened this way.
Now, his very own wife.
Once, like their very own daughter.
Is, now living in fear of disapproval.
And, may also be subjected to becoming another victim of a forced family removal.

Fear of Confusion

Daughter of a mother, whom lived a lifestyle of addictions.
Tiffany stepfather was also her, forced boyfriend in the addition.
Mom was always too drunk and passed out.
To help her daughter's fear of confusion and it was all her fault.
Embarrassed and afraid.
She had felt like no one would believe her, and all they would do is pass on judgment.
At the age of 15, is when she began running.
Packed her whole life in the briefcase and never turn back for nothing.
Boarded a Greyhound bus from New Jersey and headed straight to Cali.
½ kilo of heroin, along with $50,000 in cash.
All thanks, to her step daddy.
More than enough dough, to start a new life by far.
But, only if she was wise enough to know.
That ridin' dirty through Texas, is unforgivable law.
Sniffed out by dogs.
Hand cuffed and quickly un-boarded.
The authorities only had one concern.
And, that was the packages origin.
It wasn't the fear of being a snitch.
Young Tiffany just couldn't risk.
Being, released and being sent back to him.
She kept her mouth shut and received a three-year sentence.
In a Texas facility for the female youth, is where she started the experiencing of new feelings.
Falling in love with another female, a white girl named Mandy.
Whom, which she adored and even went on visits with her family.
By the second year into her sentence, guards were the bearers of troublesome news.
Tiffany's mother had overdosed on heroin.
Which she had found sad, but knew was way overdue.

Feelings of joy, mixed with pain, was a cocktail of emotions that she never knew.
But, overall.
Young Tiffany was no longer living in fear, of being confused.
She loved another girl and was now proud to be gay.
The life of a female rolling stone, she would begin to say.
Home will forever now be, wherever her panties would lay.

Fear of Failure

Gina grew up the oldest child, in the single parent home of her father.
Whom was hardly ever home.
Due to working multiple jobs, as the full-time provider, of two young sons and a teenage daughter.
Her mother started a new life out of town, immediately after separation and divorce.
Rumor has it.
She's living the high life now, with new love found and suffers from no type of sympathy nor remorse.
At a young age she had to pick up the slack, that her mother had left behind.
Making dinner, bottles, changing diapers, checking homework, packing lunches, plus trying to obtain her social media life.
Just, another teenage girl forced to live life grown.
In fear of failure.
She, made a promise to herself never to have kids of her own.
Until, one day her father brought home a woman he's been seeing and things became a bit of a relief.
But, Gina had to check her out for herself, in order to see if this woman truly was fit to be.
As time went by, the woman turned out to be cool.
This had become the perfect opportunity for Gina, to get herself off from studies and back into school.
Graduating with honors, at the top of her class.
Now that school is over, the real world hit back home pretty fast.
Her best friend Charlotte was now pregnant and surely she wasn't going to follow her lead.
Gina had already grew up living, in fear of failure.
Due to, too many unwanted childhood responsibilities.
No matter the path she would chose, she just knew that she had to be successful and continue to learn.
So, during law school.

Gina interned for a local top-notch hotshot firm.
Proceeding on to become, one of the greatest partners that they ever would meet.
Success and not failure.
Gina was now so you living out her dreams.

Feel the Vibrations

So much pain runs through my veins, that strike me right in the heart.
A lot of its self-inflicted.
But, some of it is from a past that others caused.
I refuse to lose, so that my soul won't ever get lost.
I could feel Electro's in every raindrop, as it pours down on me in the dark.
Whom goes there??
Show yourself !!!
I could feel eyes of thee, as if I were being stalked.
Survival is the name of the game, trying to keep from being chalked.
It's kill or be killed.
On McKinley field.
Such choice's, that so many are forced to make.
Living and dying in this game, is partly driven by fate.
Just can't trust nobody in this world, when you're constantly surrounded by snakes.
The eyes of every person, is the windows of their soul.
Just pay very close attention and the truth shall unfold.
But first feel the vibrations, of all your inner body thoughts.
Always follow your first mind and don't let it walk.
We all have gifts.
Just listen as they evolve.
Powers that be from within, that could be summoned by all.
First one must love thyself, in order to fully understand.
God lives within us all.
Every living being, child, woman and man.

 Rise

When the sun rise.
I could feel my soul shine.
One body – one mind.
One spirit, we're all a part of one whole design.
When one enters my space, I could feel energy ripples.
While speaking an unnamed language, through my thoughts.
Projecting images into others minds, in just one thought.
Living in 3 realms, all at one time.
3D visions help me see things, that to most are so blindly divine.
Looking down on the ground, most of your life.
Will have you miss many blessings, along with the truth of heights.

SPREAD MY WINGS

Today, my heart brings me to a very special state of mind.
Where I would love to spread my wings and expand my messages throughout South Central and well beyond.
I would love to touch hearts and souls across the world and become global.
To everyday people hard at work, to high-rise structures controlled by moguls.
To hustlers with Glocks and guwop grinding in bando buildings.
To teachers-preachers-single parents homes-elders-teens and children.
From the most confident person's.
To the opposite of them, whom feels so worthless.
At one point I didn't love myself.
And, I was even unbeknownst to either mine or notice.
Now, I love myself…
And, my kids give me perfect reason to stay on point and focus.
In, '92 Ice Cube said today was a good day walking through the door.
Well, as for me today is a new day and I surely will adore.
No longer worried about hitting licks.
And cashing out on scores through fences.
Today, I have faith and it's so exciting.
Because, now wealth could be built through my thoughts and writings.
Today, my life is worth so much more.
Every time opportunity knocks, I'm just going to open the door.

Just Thinking

Mix my enemies up with Hennessey , and put them all in the blenders
Fill our cups to their rims
For surely , this will be a night to remember
All of our guns are hot , but this gone be one could ass winter
Home invasions, kidnaps, arsons, receiving kickbacks and then mo' murda – mo' murder
Supposed to be legendary in these streets
But untouchable is of the unheard
My young niggas are only 14 , and just passed on a surplus
Paying tribute, they shot me 3 glocks , a vest and 2 chops
Then I'm like "word up"
But then I made sure to tell them,
Make sure to trust no one
Because "in this thing of ours," no man
Is safe under the sun
Tiny Cass E.C.I.P, said that even
The pigs could eat from a drum
I also know a hit man from Vera Cruz , Mexico
That now lives, in the heart of the city
Chopping bodies for his cartel
Dismembering shit with no pity
For 10 racks real quick
and some still believe
That if you ritualistically eat from the heart
Of another man's whole
You shall receive the extremity of energies
Along with fruits full of knowledge &
Mysterious wisdoms hidden in one's soul
Eating teriyaki – sipping supper sake with my
Yakuza bro.
100 Kawasaki's poppin wheelies in the
Rear of Maybach windows
Reclined in the back seat

Counting stacks – G 4 Gee
No room in my life for new friends
All I need on my side , is an all
Black Mack-10
Ready and willing
Please don't approach me with the bullshit
Because I'm down for the killing
As long as a Ku Klux Klan is dead , &
Hanging from my bed room ceiling
Can't forget about the early morning
Meetings , at sunrise overlooking the beach
We do this every week
So well kept in the books, smooth & discreet
So much money involved, that we can't trust nobody around us
So we do it like the swiss and switch
It up every year
Same as they receive new presidents
And we'll have hood cathedral ceiling
In all of our residence
Like dough boy's cash out
Oh yeah don't forget to vote me for president

True Worth

Never let such a thing, as simple as money control you.
Thyself's end, shall surely be a disaster.
For money is such a great slave, but yet a horrible master.
There's a difference between one's wealth and self-worth of oneself. One comes from within and the other could be stored on any shelf. Happy or sad.
Good or bad.
With or without cash, you're still the same person.
Usually change comes when dealing with people, that prey on others worthiness.
When you have it on hand, you're always in demand.
But when it's all gone, you become just another man.
Real friends don't charge by the hour, to be a presence.
They show up at your baby's shower, with cigars and baskets full of presents.
No man is willing to help the one, whom burden's the cloak of the black sheep.
But, every man has his hand out.
More than willing to help you go broke, within a week.
Life lessons learned will teach thee, to expect things of the simplest value.
Simplicity is the key to owning wealth, while still holding onto values.
Billionaires are billionaires.
Because they don't overspend on themselves.
Investments double up and true assets all pay for them self.
Make the money.
Don't let the money make you.
Master self-worth and everything else shall surely follow through.

Man's Best Friend

Kurupt said it best.
I'm only giving my own experiences and self-opinionated thoughts. On this concept.
And, so he said.
"A bitch is a bitch and a dog is a man's best friend".
I only say this.
Because two hoe's in a row, had called me a dog back when.
I thought myself, maybe they're right?
So I took a little trip, to the local dog park.
That was pretty much nearby.
Before I could even exit my vehicle, I couldn't believe my eyes.
Oh my!!!
Every chain beast resembles.
Many key factors, of the controllers of their leash.
Look there, that woman's overweight.
And, her dogs obese.
Then over to my left, what do we have here?
An aggressive looking man, of an athletic build and physique.
He's walking a Doberman Pinscher.
And, both of thee.
Are pumping fear into the hearts, of every master and pet they see. Just behind this pair.
Whom goes there?
After taking a leak.
A white chick and her pink poodle, rounds from behind a tree. Wow!!
Both are slim and trim with short haircuts.
Walks with strides full of pride and seems to be sadiddy as fuck. So the next time one of them hoes, brings them self to call me a dog. I would not think to myself maybe?
Or why?
Nor hesitate to give my hypothese and reply.
Now, armed with the perfect answer.
Due to the things I have analyzed and now realized they're right. I may be a dog!!
But, you's a bitch for life.

SPADE VS. ZELL

Real Talk

I was born of the indebted.

In the land of taxes and fees.

With hands cuffed behind my back.

I learned how to walk, with shackles on my feet.

9 digit codes are used, to mark us like cattle.

Free your mind State from Washington or end up sleepless in Seattle.

Blindfolded with American flags and scarred by the talons of bald eagles.

How come whenever we dream in the hood.

Our fantasies come out illegal.

Robbed of our culture, many countries, wealth, language, true religion and creed.

Minorities are programmed to settle for less.

While welfare checks are the hand's that feed.

We feel like we're only doing, what we have to do.

But flocking, robbing, slanging and banging don't make it no better.

Although most designers are racist.

We still pay top dollar, just to get shot over the color of sweaters.

Welcome To My World

Try out running your shadow and surely you'll end up exhausted.
Whoever knew the government was behind, a marathon of explosions in the city of Boston.
A fall guy was arrested.
But what about the backpacks and skull caps.
All of the real evidence points at.
The white faces, draped in all black.
It's impossible to catch a tiger, by gripping its tail.
I've heard those who chased the dragon.
End up high as hell.
Whom supplies the dope boys ?
Whom serves good dope fiends on my block ?
Did Obama sell the keys to the border ?
And, now the gates are unlocked ?
Houdini has nothing on El Chapo and great escapes.
From the worst Mexican prison cell.
To the most luxurious estates.
He's in the business, of birds that don't fly.
If you cook them in hot water, ice cubes will bring them back solid and then you dry.
Some praise Mal Verde and others go to church.
You can either pay tides to a preacher or double up your work.
6 days out of the week she's a freak.
But on Sunday's.
She's Christian.
While I stack green and burn trees 24/7.
Money can't buy hearts.
But I love counting them hunnits.
Gripping the steering wheel, of this Porsche.
Causes an urge to gun it.
Left fist full of dollar's.
With the right, on the wheel.
No more, locked doors.

Thoughts of a Convicted Felon

I'd rather die holding court in the field.
Give the state back their digits and continue getting that cake.
With two strikes on my jacket, there's no room for mistakes.
So I hit the 5 North, with the pass in my rearview.
No more hitting licks.
I'm pushing trees and pharmaceuticals.
These hoe's be leaning, while living their life sideways.
Purple juice and green bars.
Got these niggas nodding out.
In broad day.
I'm your pusha.
I could satisfy your needs.
Smokers are doing away with the crack pipes and switching to speed.
Crystal shard's, shine bright like diamonds.
That shit will have you climbing a ladder to forever.
The inventor of the recipe.
Was somewhat, more than clever.
Another conspiracy theory and America's occupants are its guinea pigs.
Most victims are adults.
But many started as kids.
Just enough rope, for us to hang ourselves.
With no good jobs available to us.
Crime is only thing left.
What type of life is ?
Slavery for minimum wage.
Some find life easier behind bars.
Living like animals caged.
California department of corrections and rehabilitation.
Is a mental institution.
A billion dollar industry.
But still charging inmates restitutions.
The state labels you property, numbers you and then put you up on a shelf.
Arnold took the tobacco, so lifer's will have better health.
Long live the slaves, that work for pennies.
They all have the same dreams.
Winning their appeals and a second chance at living.

Some take the easy route and purposely overdose on dog food.
First-timers pulling 16 with half, never learn their lesson's like fools.
An revolving door, with plenty of bed space.
In California they accommodate you, according to gangs and race.
Prison politics are influenced, by key holders of the system.
C.O.'s play the game too!!
That's why so many of them become victims.
Anyone can get it.
So be sure to show some respect.
Waking up on the wrong side of the bed, with an attitude.
Can get you hit in the neck.
Pushing that black tar, will boss up your living status.
Paying bills from your prison cell.
But the drug trade on the yard is savage.
Haters will drop a dime and send the goon squad right at you
It's best to have a fall guy and have another nigga working too!!
Break bread with your car.
But still keep your eyes wide open.
There's always a banana eating Caine, so you gotta stay focused.
Correctional officers are squaring off like Tyson.
Boxing, scratching and biting in the parking lots.
Narcotics profits are quadruple, behind the walls.
So they all want to make the drop.
Living beyond their means.
$100,000 trucks, cigarette boats and French vacations.
Too much flossing dog!!!
Before the indictments, was the investigations.
A prison drug ring busted, was being ran by correctional officials.
Shit was all good, just a week ago.
Until the feds came in and blew their whistles.
These type of things, happen every day in this country.
Sit a bloody steak in front of a dog.
Of course he'll eat, when hungry.
Political puppet master's in high-rises, are steadily pulling our strings.
Writing laws to protect white people.
But simultaneously destroying, my people's dream's.
I'm afraid to open my eyes.

Because I'm living in a nightmare.
Launching commercials to feed the children.
But what about those starving right here.
Rich people donate to charities.
But not 1 million ever hit my hood.
They'd rather feed animals.
Than to see Aboriginals eating good.
In my neighborhood.
There's a liquor store, on every other corner.
Death is big business and you could say it's job security for the coroner.
When local Black folks die, most don't evening have a will.
Families fighting over crumbs, that's when shit gets real.
Brothers and sisters having quarrels, over who gets to keep "Big Momma's House."
No one has come to agreement.
So it's time to sell now.
The Mexicans across the street, came with cold hard cash.
They're taking over entire communities, with extremity.
Fast!!!
Once well-established districts, are becoming impoverished.
Border protection isn't helping, their crossing regardless.
Prepare to be jobless in California, if you can't speak No Spanish!!
From Taco Bell.
To every local warehouse, they're taking full advantage.
When it comes to the underworld, it doesn't get no better.
Mexicans and Blacks.
Where I come from, just might beef forever.
And, everyone knows that Hispanics, always stick together.
While we ourselves, are still suffering from the results.
Of the Willie Lynch letter.
But in order to overcome, we must first understand.
We have inherited self-hatred.
From centuries ago passed down, from hand to hand.
It's me against the world, with my back against the wall.
All I have in this life, is my word and my balls.
Every move that I make, I know big brother is watching.
The world's under surveillance, being recorded non stopping.

I feel like Mr. Frodo.
"In The Lord of the Rings."
The power is very tempting.
But nothing in this world is free.
An eternal flame is burning.
I can see it in the sky.
I could also feel its gaze, through the reptilian slit between its eyes.
Relationships with my homies, remind me of Smeegal's.
In my face they're kind hearted.
But behind my back there evil.
And, it's always the one nigga that you'd last expect.
So when your woman lace you up.
Just be thankful for that.
Female intuition goes a long way.
I know that, I wouldn't have went to jail.
If I'd just listened to her and stayed home that day.
Always on the go and in a rush to play.
I thought that I was missing out on something and everything was the same as yesterday.
You could go around the world twice and the hood ain't gone change.
Just different players on the block.
But it's still the same old thang.
Give me got shot.
And, if!!!! If we we're a fifth we'd all be drunk.
Sabrina move to Nevada and Tommy was found dead in his trunk.

Lose, Lose, Nation

The worst thing I've ever done, was trusting another man.
I gave a dog a bone and got bit on my hand.
Under the streetlights, it doesn't pay to have a good heart.
Give your back to the wrong one and guns will spark.
Loyalty, is royalty.
But niggas be having, hidden agendas.
The game is colder than the East Coast, in the middle of December.
Mind alternating drugs.
Mixed with emotions of love, lust, jealousy and envy.
The bond is no more.
Now it's shootouts, until clips are empty.
Surrounded by snake eyes, with concealed intentions behind smiles.
Poker face the bluff.
Or you can fold out now.
Never give the full lay, your own plans can be used against you.
Always spoon feed the need to know and compartmentalize the chosen few.
In the land of the blind, the one-eyed man is King.
In the land of no pity, there's no room for peace.
In the scheme of things, we seem to be missing the bigger picture.
In the white man's world, everyone else is a nigger.
So ignorant in the sense, can't even get along with each other.
Brown is the closest thing to black.
But pride won't let us be brother's.
We make love to their sister's and they duplicate our swag.
In L.A. Mexicans are racist ass fuck.
But want to be Black, so damn bad.
I was raised in a concrete jungle, where "Only the Strong" survive.

Prisoner of My Thoughts

A psychedelic effect
On my mind and body.
A prisoner of my own thoughts.
Because I crave Maserati.
Stuck on the perception.
Of what the world sees me as.
But it's all full of deception.
Like eyes between, the slits of the ski mask.
The realest nigga that I know.
Is the man in the mirror.
Adversaries talk deceit behind my shoulders.
Because my pupils produced only fearless.
True man of Honor.
A self-made man.
Against all odds.
Like, Malcolm X.
Gun in my hands.
We're all under attack.
By plenty of unseen enemies.
Even worse than that.
So many close ones, turned frenemies.

My Own Worst Enemy

A victim of my own fault's.
Because I've caused harm to myself.
The lifestyle that I used to live, was hazardous to my own health.
Worse than tobacco.
Plus, I used to smoke cigarettes.
My own worst enemy, is what I reflect.
Playing the blame game.
Is only to be, living in a lie.
Life is a bitch and then you die.
The weight on my shoulders.
Has " No Limit."
I'm " In Too deep."
So I guess that, I just have to deal with it.
So much pain in my eyes, mixed with so much love.
Like losing your soulmate.
For another little bitch you fucked.
Trusting a friend.
Just to get, stabbed in the back.
Committing a crime and getting caught in the act.
Time in a cell.
Makes one appreciates what's gone.
Thoughts are reminisced, of all thy did wrong.
If only I could.
"Turn Back The Hands of Time."
I would do things different and lead a way better life.
I've been in the county a whole year and still got to go to prison.
This ain't living.
It's more like, merely existing.
I have kids in the world and I miss them dearly.
True my troublesome ways, could use some healing.
So I pray, for "Better Dayz."
While down on my knees.

My celly is Muslim.
So he face's the East.
Every day is the same, just as the last.
Lord willing.
My future overcomes my past.

Zell of the Jungle

Born with a heart cold as ice, but solid as gold.
A gift and a curse.
For Better or worse.
Breastfed by a mother wolf, so in my mouth piece.
Are sharp teeth.
Just another man-child raised by killas, go-gettas and silverback gorillas.
I grew up on the Eastside of my street.
Inside of an urban jungle, molding out of concrete.
Had to gut me a snake and gator.
Just for a belt, along with fresh pair of sneaks.
A child of the sun.
But on late nights.
I often howl and growl at the Moon.
King of " Hamburger Hill," as I'm overlooking my city.
True warrior like Hannibal and keep a fleet of elephants with me.
Beating on my chest, as I serenade the jungle.
That's how I bust Jane.
The day she brought me, George's bundle.
Swinging on Vine trees from my block, to your street.
As everyone admires my crown made of emeralds, diamonds, gold and rubies.
Even in dim lights.
I sparkle and glisten.
Nigga!!!
Now, listen!!!
Am I speaking loud enough?
Can you hear me clearly?
I don't need a bodyguard.
Because that oven on my hip and two shooters are with me.

Don't tempt me!!!
Nor, test me!!!
Because I will kill you tonight and then bail out in the morning.
I, Am.
" Zell of The Jungle "
My, nigga…
& this is your warning.

Night-mariKKKa

Last night I had, another Night-mariKKKa.
But first let me tell you what happened.
Before I woke up yellin' bruh.
The sky fell down first and then suddenly the weight of the world was on my shoulders.
As I tunnel visioned down memory lane and realize the game was over.
Since when did respect, become purchasable by stacks in the streets.
Not to mention so many cooperating and getting paid by the police.
I grew up with a cat, who ended up changing the tune of our cadence.
Word was he had a camera in his charm and had us all under surveillance.
In a dog eat dog world, a close friend with slit your throat.
Then console your widowed wife.
Real talk.
No joke.
The hood was so hot.
I saw heat waves on the block.
Cuz was wanted for murder, when the pigs kick doored in his spot.
Tattoo's, prison yards, dead homies, drugs and liquor.
In a white man's world, everyone else is a Nigger.
The first metropolitan of Mexico, was an Olmec creation.
Indigenous Amurakans and Africans together built a nation.
In the California prison system Mexicans and Aboriginals hate one another.
You would think minority groups, would get along like brothers.
In the streets of LA the racial wars continue.
Candlelight's, bald heads, Cortez, Chuck's, bandanas and cocktails through windows.
Nazis hide in plain sight and laugh at our ignorance.
A majority-white jury bench and a pale-faced judge was my last court appearance.

Better Dayz

Born to a princess.
But not yet a queen.
Wasn't yet a woman, my mother was a teen.
Daddy drove a Caddy and hustled that caine.
He also made sure there was Jordans on my feet and every year Christmas had came.
I remember my first bike was a blue BMX.
And my favorite restaurant, was a liquor store my aunt worked at.
They also sold my favorite hamburgers, all the way in the back.
Long Beach avenue and Vernon was the intersection we had reside.
A big pink house.
Right across the street from the train tracks, where many people had died.
Trying to Hitch rides off the locomotive, was the cause losing their limbs.
Bodies torn in half lost hands, heads and brims.
I was raised in a zone of time.
When crack dealers had their prime.
Violence due to drugs, was at an all-time high.
Crip's and blood's, shooting gun, bustin' heads.
While drug kingpins were going FED.
Mac tens and 211 suits.
Battering ram Sam and his crew.
Knocking down doors.
Trampling through living room floors.
Stomping Black asses, with their big black boots.
Parents sent to prisons.
While their youngin' children went to the system.
That's if their grandparents, couldn't get them.
Brenda's got a Baby.
Uncle's shooting dope, living shady.
Crackheads doing rapes and stealing from their own families.
Breaking into houses.

People raising their kids behind bars, that our government calls public housing.
The white men smiling.
While local gangs are killing each other and recruiting youth by the thousands.
My father found a wife and tried to move me to a better part of the city.
It's true what they say.
You can take the boy out the hood.
But, this Crip shit still lived in me.
Caught up for my first burglary, when I was only 11.
Before then I got away with, at least like 7.
Started off shoplifting from the Carson mall.
FUBU, Tommy Hilfiger, Guess, and Boss.
Stealing liquor from stores.
To drug dealers we sold.
Taught how to chop rocks and watch the game unfold.
Came across a few guns.
Then started bustin' for fun.
Rosebud's of youthful criminals.
This is how crime spree's begun.
At the age of 12.
I ended up lockdown for robbery in a juvenile cell.
18 months I was gone.
A young loec on his own.
Never did no cryin'.
Ever since then.
I felt like I was full grown.
Me and Blackwell, put the smash on rivals.
The fittest.
Of the fittest.
In a place where only the Strong was survival.
Delecia had sent me pictures, holiday cards and letters every week.
Until I found my way back to the streets.
Since then I spent a few years in C.Y.A.
Then even more in the C.D.C.
Crippin' ain't ever been easy.
Especially, when you're from

N-H-E-C-B-C-G
All of the time and years that I've lost, could never be replaced.
As a personal promise to myself.
I'm going to raise my children in a better way.
Like Tupac, I pray for us all.
Please true Lord
Let there be.
Better days.
Better daze.
Better dayz.

Me Against The World

Up against the ropes and against All odds.
Assassination of character, all built on lies.
False slanderous tongues, with comes hatred from another man.
These this motherfuckers fear the capabilities, of my well thought-out master plan.
I'm guessing because in the eyes of those that envy.
I'm such a renaissance man.
Deployed here to Earth.
From the highest, of all highs almighty.
A man on a mission, sent to save the Lost.
Reign supreme over envious-jealous ones and the weaknesses of the all.
Infiltrators try to convert, but they're nothing like I.
So contrary to me.
Because I'm so one of a kind.
Only acceptance, invitations and initiations for real and never the fake.
High-rise buildings resemble blades of grass and you hatin' ass niggas be slithering snakes.
Cut the head off the Cobra and the body shall surely die.
Just before I bury its head into the Earth.
Along with all of their poisonous hatred and lies.

AmeriKKKa Hates U.S.

So much power between two hands.
Too much power, for just one man.
Crushing entire buildings, in just one thought.
Change the weather in just one sneeze-one cough.
Have a few rounds and cheer's at the bar.
Then travel a few light-years…
First stopping at the moon and then on to Mars.
None of your business…
On my trip, what I had saw.
As far as, you know.
I was in Hollywood, because I was struck by A-Star.
Can't hide in this world.
Because everywhere you go.
Siri knows where you are.
Ping your cell phones, Bluetooth and Google Earth your cars.
Can't forget about secret indictments and government phone taps.

Gots to be more careful about what you say and who you're saying it too.
Informants are everywhere.
From the bottom of the totem pole, to the highest chains of food.
Charles Crosby told on himself...
Without ever being caught for his dirty deeds, while out paying his dues.
Having Griselda Blanco as a girlfriend and pin pal...
Had just become a way bigger bite, than he could ever digest nor chew.
Very sweetly asking him to be involved, in her plan to kidnap John f Kennedy.
They would then be able to barter his return.
In exchange, for her freedom from captivity.
Charles already had known...
That the US government would spare no expense, for the recapture or death of the cocaine Queen.
Also on the chopping block would be his own head.
For the withholding information that led to this scheme.
These are the same people that waterboard terrorist and break down global factions to find out who? Is who?
Watergate a president, for getting too big for his shoes.
Why are they always talking about global warming?
Because if the water ever rises...
My folks already learned from Katrina, what the government is going to do.
I assume Amerikkka's ghettos, will be left sunken and abandoned.
Or do you still think that FEMA, is here to protect you?
I almost want to laugh...
Because it all sounds like a big joke.
In New Orleans, besides the wrath of Katrina?
Who do you think set off them bombs?
That made them loud explosive sounds, before those levees broke.
Then when survivors tried crossing the bridge that ended in Mississippi.
Pale-faced cops click! Clacked!!
Shotguns and sent them people back to their now underwater city.

Nothing is accidental…
Tragedies are a game of global control, caused by people with credentials.
That target minority groups, always as planned.
These same tactics are also used, with the making of new laws.
Instill fear in every woman and anger every man.
Cause rioting, looting and confusion.
The more that we try to fight back, the more we still end up losing.
If you ever want to know what's next.
Purchase tickets at your local box office.
Or watch it all unfold at home, over dinner, a bottle of wine and Netflix.

Self-Destruction

We've come so far as a race, nationality and Creed.
Although, so many of us are so blinded by greed.
March 14th 1984 in the city of Los Angeles, is when and where I was conceived.
My initials are even engraved on the side, of the big red brick building.
That should have been a sign to my parents, family and the world.
Shit was just about to get real then.
C.H.W.
California hospital of the West.
And, as far as I'm concerned.
The year 1984 in my city, was one of the best.
First off as a gift to the world.
I was born again.
Also, forever marked in world history.
You have the 1984, Los Angeles Olympics.
Which by the way.

Took place right down the street, from the home I live in.
At that time, from what I know.
The ghetto economy was boomin'.
So that means, plenty of dollars were being made.
Most probably sold dope.
But I'm sure pimpin', had hoe's on the blades.
Those whom chose to deal drugs, at this time had it good for sure.
Because America had a president.
That wanted his country operating, off of a high so pure.
It was nothing for a hustler to buy a Mercedes, Ferrari or even a Rolls-Royce.
Every day wear Gucci suits, plus dress their kids in Jordans and velour.
Gold around everybody's neck.
Rolex watches and bracelets.
8 ball jackets and brick phones for ballers.
Bamboo earrings and biker shorts for the hood rats, waiting at home for the local d-boy too call her.
Back then the police, were so lame to the game.
Always pulling dealers over in fancy cars.
Poppin' the trunk and still overlooking the caine.
Good clientele, made you at high roller.
Sports figures, movie stars, doctors and lawyers.
Then things all went South, when came in the war on drugs.
The batter ram came to town and they started locking up thugs.
Now look at all the bullshit that Ronald Reagan and George W. Bush had done.
Started an internal war with their own country and were the biggest kingpins.
So there should be no questions, about who won.
From the beginning.
It was all out war on Copper-colored people.
A plan that was thoroughly thought of and constructed till it's ending.
What about the broken up families?
Due to mother's and father's, going to prisons.
I guess it was also a good year.
For the department of children and social services building's.
Food for thought.
Now, was it really really worth all of this?

Crackheads of the 80s.
Plenty of " Brenda's got a Baby".
Does white America even give a fuck, about our people.
I seriously doubt.
That we'll ever be considered their equals.
On top of all that.
In this deadly game of life that we play.
The US government, uses our own people's against us.
Just like pawn's.
Directly related to the situation at hand.
Somewhere, was a Black man entwined.
In which, at this time.
A lot of inner-city youth, had surely idolized.
And, today by a lot of rappers still glorified.
Rick Ross.
Also known as freeway Rick.
Who was our governments inside man.
Receiving the mother loads, of Nicaraguan contraband.
Fresh off of planes and boats.
I'm not sure if he ever dealt with heroin.
But, for sure the man had all of the coke.
Some would say, that he was a killer of his own kind.
Because the dope that he sold, had caused a new wave of Black human genocide.
While others would say.
That he paved the way, for ghetto superstars of this time.
But, to federal agents, correctional officers and in some case's many of the prisoners.
He was labeled a rat.
Because, although it be the government.
He still told on his connect.
I'm sure over all of the time that he did.
He had a lot of regrets.
Made himself one, with his higher power.
In return received a chance to reflect and repent.
It's still sad to say.
How his own country helped him, fuck himself.
Then locked him up for their actions.

Reflection

Born a lost soul, in the city of Lost Angel's.
Now looking at my life, from different points of views and all sorts of angles.
Searching for another soul, to console my heart.
In pursuit without a flashlight, but still finds me In the dark.
My life is a roller coaster, so I'm strapped in with nowhere to hide.
No place to run, so I'm in for the ride.
A lot of lessons taught for me, has been a lot of lessons learned.
Due to constant confinement.
So many years out of my life, has been adjourned.
It's time to do better for my kid's and gain wealth without lick's.
Through discipline and persistence.
I feel I could pursue, a true lifestyle of happiness.
My biggest asset is myself, so I now practice good health.
As soon as one stops learning, thee may as well prepare themselves for death.
Cash might make you rich.
But, wisdom and knowledge is the shit.
Had to find time to love myself, before I gave my heart to another bitch.
I offer a heart pure like gold and unconditional is my love.
Energetic as a dove.
So, heavenly.
You can feel my presence from above.

Bullets Don't Have No Names

Hell is hot and the game is cold.
For the price of fame, many will sale their souls.
Suicide by cop.
Because he wasn't going back to the pen.
Tiny Cass E.C.I.P.
Died with an AK in his hands.
Murder by the numbers, these pigs are killing our peoples.
It's time to strike back and even out the score to equal.
Trading guns for gift cards, is a foolish act in itself.
In the case of martial law.
How would you protect yourself?
Giving away your rights to bear arms, for Thanksgiving turkey dinner
When you could get a better deal.
From your local thugs and drug dealers.
No one listens or pays attention.
Until it's all too late.
We're prisoners in our own country, being ran by cold-blooded snakes.
Who's going to police the pigs?
That still shoots when your hands are up?
"We need power to the people!!!"
Because our government's corrupt.
Speak too freely and end up marked for death.
Deliverance of powerful speeches, killed Malcolm Luther X. Conspiracy theories, targeted victims and fall guys.
So much potential, in colorful pigmentation.
But they refuse to let us rise.
Aboriginals are full of love.
But the world hates my race.
The world without color would be such a dreadful place.
Unable to see the picture clearly, we all seem to be so blind.
But if we open real wide.
We'll realize we're living behind enemy lines.

Lie to through politicians and control by an unseen force.
Tracked down by facial recognition and put the death with no remorse.
A government "Terminator" world army, on the prowl for the resistance.
So stop taking incriminating photos.
Because Facebook is do-it-yourself surveillance.
A closet full of guns.
But in the streets you're naked.
Plus you just I.G.'d one hundred racks.
How are you going to protect it?
Chris Brown's home was invaded, with his aunt at gunpoint.
Trying to make gang friends in L.A.
This ain't what you really want.
Maybe next time he'll be kidnapped and held for ransom.
Of course not for chump change.
More like something healthy and handsome.
A homeboy will steal from your mother, slap your sister and fuck your bitch.
Pull you down like a crab in the barrel, just to get rich.
Ask no questions and hear no lies.
You could always find the truth.
By the way, one dots their eyes.
Like teacher, like pupil, like father, like son.
To live and die in L.A.
Us to live and die by the gun.

Pillow Talk

When you get born to win, it's impossible to lose.
Time to turn up the jazz and do away with the blues.
There's a king in my heart, of blood that's pure and Royal.
I need a queen in my life, bonded to be loyal.
Someone to share an estate, overlooking the coast.
My best friend till the end, like food to my soul.
No deep dark secrets we, confide each other.
A bond over brothers, to be share with my lover.
I used to think I had friends, until they prove to be different.
All that my brother's keeper shit, helped I see my weakness. Whispers over my shoulders, were brought to my attention.
For them to penetrate my ears, just wasn't the motive of their intentions.
News travels pretty fast, for those who pillow talk with hoe's.
You should have trust no bitch, like that saying goes.
I guess keeping it real, isn't in your field.
I just hope them bitches you trustin', give you a round of applause full of claps.
It's not easy being one of the last, of a dying breed.
Because I don't even got to hate, for niggas to hate on me. Whenever my bitch asked questions, you always told the truth. These hoes ain't loyal, because of niggas like you.
Your dumb ass still didn't get the pussy!!!
But, I'd bet it will hurt your little feelings, if you ever found out that I been fucked, the one that you're calling your boo.

9-2-5

I work hard for the money, but it's only minimum wage.
Got me feeling like it's indentured servitude, doing the work of a slave.
Managers and supervisors don't even fit the criteria.
Could care even less about hiding, their racist facial expressions on the exterior.
Forklift and electric pallet jacks carrying heavy loads to the back.
All I do is sweep and carry boxes around because last time I got hurt like that.
I was fresh out the pen making $12 an hour off of which I couldn't survive.
So I went to pest control school and passed the course with flying colors.
But, for my criminal past and mishaps the State board surely denied.
Devastated by this news and to make matters worse, they just cut off my disability.
But, I'm a born Hustler.
So, I hit all of the local auctions up and distributed cars all over the city.
Ran that game for just about nine months and on the side was graveyard shift doing security.
No guard card but I packed a knife and a gun.
But, if I had to use either of them.
I'd probably would be just another parolee, once again on the run.
Everything else seems so unpromising to me and I know that I can't go back to being a crook.
So, I slowed down on doing security and everything else and started focusing more on publishing my book.

IN THE DARK

Let's Take A Stand

Lurking beyond the shadows, is a team of secret agents.
They want the world on lockdown, when we're already under surveillance.
The use of excessive force, is only bait for their trap.
White cops killing Black men.
We're obviously under attack.
The military is already in place.
But war is not the answer.
The system wants us to riot.
So they can kill us off like cancer.
A police state with curfews and being jailed without trial.
Activation of concentration camps.
In mass they want to see us bow.
Rioting is not revolutionary.
But rather reactionary.
Because it invites defeat.
Words much brilliantly put.
By the late Dr. Martin Luther King.
His success was through peaceful protest.
Created through non-violence and determination.
Indeed he was murdered.
But first was able to put an end to segregation.
We need to set aside differences.
That causes our division.
All of the manufactured irrelevance's, politics, race, culture, income brackets and religion.
Not by rejecting our beliefs.
Just no longer letting them be weapons of our very own separation.
We're All in This together.
While the challenge is to avoid any acts of desperation.
Not stealing from each other, looting, rioting or even simply looking away.
What's not your problem now.
You just may become a victim of another day.

They're not targeting Muslims, Jews, Black people, Mexicans, middle class and so on.
They're after all of U.S.
Picking off different groups, until we're all gone.
"Am I my brother's keeper?"
"I am," my brother.
We need to get re-organized in our own communities and stop with all of the killing each other.
How could we be enemies?
With so much in common.
Conversations with rival gang members in prison.
Over summer sausage, cheese squeeze, refried beans, chips and Ramen's.
The worst nightmare of the system, is in our non-cooperation.
Refusal to pay taxes, in the sum of large denominations.
Refusing to leave homes, when the bank foreclosed on them.
Because of an economic collapse.
Caused by the same banks, that foreclosed on them.
This needs to be done in mass, with the support & love from one another.
Not just fighting for your freedom.
But also the freedom of others.
Those not immediately affected, need to support those who are.
The system couldn't cope with this, being done on a massive scale by far.
None of this shall be done.
In the spirit of rage, hostility nor violence.
But more along the lines of love, joy and laughter all the while smiling.
Refusal to join a military, that wishes to enslave our people.
Just another monkey in the uniform, we will never be their equals.
Soldiers don't have any power, it's the uniform that does.
Doing the bidding and dirty work, for a group of government thug's.
Frozen into non-action.
By ignorance and fear.
Starring us right in the face the conspiracy is unfolding here.
It's we the people, whom has all of the power.
The sooner we unify, acts against us shall be devoured.

There's no need, to hold out for a hero.
We are the chosen one's.
The consciousness of the people.
With great strength and courage.
We can overcome this oppression.
Refusing fear and intimidation.
While casting off the chains of suppression.
We need not let worries.
Like consequences get in our way.
Because our children and grandchildren.
Lives and futures are all at stake.

Overcoming The Illusion

Living in a lost world.
Blocked from the most high of consciousness.
Genetically manipulated, body-computers.
Electrochemical destabilization through food and drink additives.
Robot like mind control.
Has the human race, on our knee's.
We're all prisoners of perception.
Now it's time for us to break free.
The most power in a pyramid, is in the masses at the bottom.
The weakest point is the capstone.
So why do we continually follow?
Their plan is manipulation and separation.
Through haves and have nots.
Income brackets and religion.
If enough people come together.
The conspiracy cannot continue without the division.
Look within self subconsciously and enter new areas of understanding.
You've already made the choice.
Now you have to understand it.
Our five senses keeps us grounded.
When we're really of no limitation.
Connected universally eternal as one.
First you must open yourself to the vibrations.
The being of everywhere and everything.
With no such thing as time.
Start's with letting go of emotional and mental blocks.
Opening self to a higher consciousness of mind.
Remember you didn't come here to make the choice.
You've already made it.
Challenge's become opportunities.
In the world of "The Matrix."
Transformation of thyself and focused intuitions on freedom of mind state.

In a search for true self.
"The Lion Sleeps No More."
Once awake.
In order for the new to manifest, we must transition from old energy.
You're here to try and understand.
Why you made the choice to be?
Necessary events need to happen, for experiences to be created.
Intuition see's life from many forms.
While body-mind is subject to be manipulated.
Life is a pre-planned journey.
But we deviate with intent.
The challenge is making your intent and pre-planned journey synchronistic.
The combination of the two, can make your life go smoothly.
Most people spend their whole lives, with intentions at war with their journey.
The decision to do something.
When intuitive energy want's something else.
The intuition to do more.
Instead of settling for less.
Stepping out of mind and into higher levels of awareness.
Breaking free from manipulated illusions guided into personal and collective freedom in wellness.
We are what we eat.
While we attract what we experience.
Changing what we don't like.
By changing ourselves, gives one deliverance.
Freedom's just another word, for nothing left to lose.
Some people have to lose the world.
In order to get away, from the matrix of the Moon.
The darkest hour can be, just before the rise of dawn.
Life as an ugly duckling.
To the rebirth of an elegant swan.

History of Shadows

Highly advanced civilizations and universal lost planets.
Sunken continental land masses.
Lumeria and Atlantis.
The tale of Noah and the great flood.
Same story about Gilgamesh, has been written on clay tablets of mud.
Different cultures around the world, all serenade the same rhyme.
Man lived like god's, in a "Land before time."
United by love.
Living together with mutual confidence, among define being's.
Animals spoke through telepathy.
Understanding and conversing with human beings.
Then came extraordinary geological upheavals, fire-breathing mountains and boiling sea's.
The falling of skies, land rising and sinking.
Lost of great continents and the flipping over of Earth.
The Sun and the Moon disappearing.
Ice covered rocks and then came the darkness.
A wall of water, sweeping across the whole world.
"The fall of Man."
Caused by a cataclysm and fantastic flood.
A tidal wave that produced pressures, of 2 tons per square inch.
Mammoths embedded in ice and whole region's Frozen in an instant.
Shifting of tectonic plates, caused earthquakes and volcano fires.
Mu is located in a region called.
"The Ring of fire."
Submerged building's, stone circles, pyramids, walls and roads.
The Bermuda triangle of Atlantis and rediscoveries of intersecting worlds.
Beyond capabilities of modern technology.
Mystery structures appear all around the globe.
1000 ton bricks perfectly placed, thousands of years ago.
Pyramids, temple's, stone circles and standing stones.
All lined up precisely with the star formations.

Aligned in relationship to each other, around the world in deep rotation.
They credit Franklin and Edison.
When electric batteries were found in ancient Egyptian tombs.
Even bullets were discovered, in prehistoric animal bones.
Some 3 billion years old.
Behold South African perfect metal sphere's.
Then from 5.5 million years ago.
An imprint of a modern shoe, with a heel.
Humanoid footprints were also discovered, among dinosaur remains.
When came these rediscoveries.
Why didn't history textbooks change?
Sumerians came from Kemet and Sumer is now Iraq.
More than 240,000 years dated.
Is how far their Kings go back.
Obsession with interbreeding of bloodlines, to keep the genetic code conductive.
Controlling government, business, banking and media.
In order to keep their power structured.
Breeding with others.
Would only cause them to become diluted.
The purity of Royal blood, will then become polluted.
The empire of Babylonians traveled great distances by land and sea.
With destinations in Europe.
But particularly Britain at around 3,000 BC.
Traveling and settling.
Far and wide.
Sumerians, Egyptians, Danaans and Phoenicians.
We're basically the same people's, with agendas of somewhat similar missions.
Mystery Schools, Secret Societies, Arch Sorcerers and Black Magicians.
The takeover of countries.
While seeking of shamans and ancient knowledge carriers to kill them.
Then came introductions of religions.
Mainly for mind and perception control.

They hoarder ancient wisdom and left the masses ignorant as troll's.
World leaders are puppets and we hallucinate freedom.
Republicans and Democrats.
Are all ran by the same people.
Doesn't matter who you vote for.
Because regardless, the government still gets in.
Shadow people pulling strings, with their unseen hands.
Doing whatever they're told to do, all on need to know basis.
Best way to keeping secrets.
Is hiding information.
Through compartmentalization.
Global wealth being ran by, a group of international bankers.
An invisible world government.
Has U.S. going down like anchors.
Wearing us down with strategies, over long periods of time.
Wolves in sheep's clothing, coming after our hide's.
Four unions under one dictatorship, is the emergence of globalization.
Pyramids controlling, other pyramids.
Is the pyramid of manipulation.
Say bye to the free trade (NAFTA), and hello to the American Union.
United States, Canada and Mexico.
A microchip population in ruins.
Exploiting the poorest people's, to produce products for pennies.
The dismantling of trade barriers.
To move products wherever, without facing financial penalties.
The suppression of cures, to slow down population growth.
Monitoring the food supply and it would be illegal to privately grow.
School hours will be longer.
But the youth would learn less.
Encouragement of homosexuality and reproduction without sex.
Long established neighborhoods and communities.
Will be destroyed by unemployment and mass immigration.
Some books would disappear from libraries.
Controlling who has access to information.
Changing of the Bible and keywords through revisions.
Elimination of private doctors and blending of religions.

The need to build more jails.
Using crime to manage society.
Implanted ID cards, shifting of population's and economies.
Restrictions on travel and televisions that watch you.
Private home ownership would disappear.
Then comes encouragement of drug abuse.
Changing laws to promote chaos and a jungle like atmosphere.
While the use of terrorism, has the masses living in fear.
It's obvious we the people, are fully under attack.
Opening our third eye through consciousness.
Is the only way to fight back.

Stars, Quasars, Pills and Potions

Behind enemy lines.
My country tis of thee.
Living in an illusion called the land of the free.
In fear of slaughter, like cattle in a herd.
But still pray every night and keep faith in the world.
Hunger for the truth.
While our government feed's us lie's.
Picking up pennies and missed the change in the sky.
For pressing the real.
JFK got assassinated.
Then a fake moon landing, by Kubrick was created.
All the while Pyramid's in Egypt, have mirror images beyond the stars.
Similarities between the Moon and Darth Vader's death Star.
A silver chariot, led by 10 white horses.
As a figure of speech.
Better yet, let's make that metaphoric.
The Suns forgiving.
But never is the Moon.
Pythons lie in wait.
Around the earthly shadows they loom.
The Great flood, biblical rain's, 40 days and 40 nights.
Did Noah transport an Arc?
Or was it really a spacecraft flight?
Some cultures recognize a time, that was before Selene.
The Greek goddess of the moon.
Came after a people called the Proselene.
Once upon a time androgynous, then became genetic manipulation.
Banished from Mpalalatsani.
Men and women were separated.
"The Garden of Eden."
Found 640 light years away.
While "The Tree of Life"
Are the one's at, a higher conscious state.
Built by star god's, from the city of the Doomed Satellite.

Nazca lines in Peru, could only be seen from sky heights.
We're under attack and can't even see the war.
Eye's wide shut…
How uneven is the score?
Bioterrorism and mass genocides through deadly vaccinations.
Developed in laboratories, for the purpose of depopulation.
Can't trust my own physician.
Because he sold his soul.
For bonus compensation and lavish paid vacations I'm told.
Tullio Simoncini was disbarred.
While doctors under orders excelled.
Prescribing cures for the masses I guess?
Is punishable by jail.
Ancient Egyptians knew the answer's.
To ridding the body of cancer.
So then why is Uncle Sam, one of the main disease planter's?
Why heal the world?
When healthy people don't pay medical bills?
It's big business in the sick…
Or at least that's how our government feels.
Cancer is a fungus.
Yeast-like organism.
Caused by Candida.
In which small amounts, even live inside of healthy people.
When it begins to morph.
Is the problem.
But Cancer cannot manifest, in an alkaline environment.
What about our children?
Who's going to save the babies?
Injected with 25 chemical cocktail vaccinations.
All before the age of 2, just sounds crazy.
Isn't their immune systems still growing and advancing?
Before full development.
Already experiencing dismantling.
There's no war on drugs.
It's more like a war for profits.

U.S. government dealers, against Street pharmacist pockets.
From CVS, to the trap's.
It's all the same old thang.
What they don't tell you is.
Ritalin's a derivative of cocaine.
" Say No, To Drug's "
But gladly accept our prescriptions.
Adderall, Concerts, Metadata, Focalin, Strattera and of course Ritalin.
Doctor's prescribed these to children, with signs of ADHD.
Pill's given the same effects as, users on methamphetamines.
What about the side effects?
Like insomnia, nervousness, nausea, vomiting and violence?
Voices in their heads won't stop.
Now they're going mad and begging for silence.
What about the ending results?
Teens involved in killing sprees.
Jeopardizing students, teachers and staff.
From elementary, high School, onto Universities.
Risperdal was used on political prisoners, by the Soviet Union.
Its purpose was extracting information.
So tell me again?
Why is this shit now being prescribed, to America's children?
One and eight of American youth, are taking any one of these drugs.
We're raising generation's, of emotionless Cubs.
With they're doped-up, zombie mind states.
They can't even follow, the most simplest of instructions.
We're putting trust in a government, that's so full of corruption.
We're all dying slow.
While they're killing U.S. softly.
Producing genetically modified foods.
Murdered by potatoes and broccoli.
Which also produce toxins, allergies, new diseases, nutritional problems, antibiotic-resistant diseases and cancer-causing agents.
Microwavable quick fix dinners.
Now is that still that still your favorite?
Or what about food additives?

Like aspartame artificial sweetener.
The mind-altering sugar, that causes kids to fidgeter.
Now they can't stay still…
Attention, Deficit, Hyperactivity, Disorder?
Pop the top on the pills, just like the doctor ordered.
One can of cola, contains 9 teaspoons of sugar.
Drink too many and find out what different body functions trigger.
Consumption of refined sugar, leads to bad health.
Causes depression, cancer, coronary heart disease, dementia and eventually death.

Sweet Land of Misery

Let's take a look at the world, from a darker beings perspective.
Is it more than a probability?
That we're born and raising our children in a country, where we'll never be respected?
Nor, protected?
As if there is no such thing, as civil rights.
Or even laws at all.
Those on probation and parole are the biggest targets behind Babylon's walls.
As if awaiting permanent detainment, or death inside of the lion's den.
Officers of the law, are the Lions.
Awaiting to maul and devour us all.
Now, let's try to walk in the shoes of Trayvon Martin.
Whom was murdered.
Unarmed.
By a neighborhood watchman.
For being highly pigmented, argumentative and wearing a hoodie in the dark.
Ever since the acquittal of Zimmerman, he's had plenty of run-ins with the law.
Two domestic disputes.
One while brandishing a weapon and also threatening to shoot.
Then turn around and had a confrontation in the airport with Boosie "Bad Azz" Hatch.
Called him a Nigger!!!
Then took a flight, good night for that.
Now, two years later the police are on their own murdering spree.
Aboriginals and Hispanic men are being hunted for game.
Welcome to this, "sweet land of misery."
No liberty and No justice at all.
Cops are killing citizen and receiving desk duties.
For these acts.
Entire precincts need to be held for scrutiny.
In, Houston.

You can't even go to school, be Black and free.
Jordan Baker was a 26 year-old Aboriginal, whom had attended a local University.
So much for higher learning.
I guess deep in the South.
Confederate flags still fly high, on the side of crosses burning.
Pale faces want to see us "black-faced" and begging for lives.
Out on the East Coast, on an Island called Staten.
Six children lost their father and Ramsey Orta had to watch his dear friend die while police jacked him.
In loving memory, of his friend's sake.
Hopefully they find Justice.
Because, he caught it all on tape.
43 year old Eric Garner continued to yell, that he couldn't breathe until his very last breath.
As the police had him in a chokehold, that caused his slumberous death.
Is this the sentence in New York for pedaling loose cigarettes?
Execution for a crime, that's not even felonist.
Ramsey then put himself on house arrest.
Because of the NYPD's consistency, of their common death threats.
What this sounds like to me.
Is that he needs some Cali tree, a .223 and a Teflon plated vest.
Before he end up being the next, to be laid to rest.
In the St. Louis suburban community of Ferguson, Missouri.
Mike Brown and a friend while walking home from the store.
A police officer had made rude comments.
In which Mike and his friend continued walking as they ignored.
The racist pale-faces pursuing them, took this as a sign of disrespect.
So they popped open their squad car doors, with weapons drawn, aiming for chest.
Mike Brown screamed, "My hands are up don't shoot."
They shot him anyway.
Now, it's national headline NEWS.
Back on the west coast, in Los Angeles City.
Inside the heart, of my very own neighborhood.
"The land of no pity."

Right there in the middle of the Pac.
Is where Shootin' Newton patrols, investigates, build false reports, prey and attacks.
Guns out, shoot first and aiming for killing.
A tradition of this secretive cult, whom are known for pillage.
And if you shall survive shots, from their government issued Glocks.
Cold lies will be told on the stand.
As you pose unwantedly, for their cameraman.
Before God one hand will be raised, followed by the slam of a gavel.
Like a blue ribbon, watch time of unravel.
At a point, in time.
Ezell Ford, was a friend of mine.
But it's sad to say, at the tender age of 24.
Officers of hate.
Had ended his rhyme, for no reason.
Not here to protect and serve.
Their gangs banger's in uniforms, leaving bodies dead on the curb.
Betrayal of there being sworn in and should all be charged with treason.

The Trap

Quitting is not the same as, quitting while you're ahead.
Greed is surely destruction, so settle for success instead.
In this sweet land of misery, it seems my people will never see freedom.
Living in a world where liberty.
Is nothing more than an illusion, where I come from.
Awaken from the American dream, by the slave bell that rung.
Locked up for burglary, in a land founded by thieves.
Archaeologists are paid millions, to steal and rewrite his-story.
Become, the best at anything and this government will make you a pawn.
Disagree to enslavement and you'll be dead by Dawn.
When I was in court, it was the same people against me.
Well who's going to protect my people, from the corruption of them very same police.
If you ask me, their living above the law.
Murder a so called minority, woman or man.
Then receive desk duties, resign or even retire while receiving a pension.
Biggest gang in the world, Nationwide in attendance.
Violating people's rights and even arresting the innocent.
And, you wonder why?
We call you fags and pigs.
They took the cigarettes and weights, out of all the pen's.
In the California department of the P.I.A.
They want their lifer's, to live longer.
Because, the dead don't pay.

The Beginning of the End

Today the world had heard Dr. King speak of his dreams through a national speech
But, do you think we'll ever have peace?
Just the other night
All black on black, red, and blue lights
Black and white cars, came
Pale face's who were racists
Black Billy clubs against, all-black faces
Powerful water hoses to spray thee and
Whoever tried to run were chased by dogs with sharp teeth.
What type of world is this?
"Let start a riot"
Through window's throw bricks
Jump in and grab plenty of shit
Burn down every building unowned
By black's

Thoughts of a Convicted Felon

"They can't catch us all"
So, enough of us will get away with that
We could use our proceeds, to bail
Out our brothas who were apprehended
But NO!!! Everybody would rather catch up
On bill's, furnish they house or go buy Benz's
You can't love your brotha until you start lovin yourself
And what's wealth? If you're all alone, with nobody else.
It's true you have to have your own vision
Just make sure, a part of your plan
It not only your new family, but also
All of your children
And, everyone who has been there for you
"REAL RECOGNIZE REAL"
So, always stay true to the ones you love, and those who love you
In northern California due to the circumstance of struggle, a
Few local heroes were made.
Hovey P. Newton and Bobby Seale together
Picked up the slack, that their people had strayed
They did a lot of good in their neighborhood
Taught indigenous people about their rights and for those same people's
Freedom, they'd even risk their lives
All the while making sure that before school
The local youth were full
Fuck screaming " no justice 'no peace !!!"
They Pulled shotguns on racist faces, hiding
Behind their badges of the O.P.D.
I bet they wouldn't dare come with that dumb shit
Whenever they entered the 69/65village
Ran by a black man
With a master plan
Felix Mitchell was his name
And selling dope was his game
His rivals had no win with him, so the federal government had to end his reign
A true to life, New Jack City Boss

Someone who really walked the walk and talked the talk
One of the first, to every in Oakland
Become a drug kingpin
Even bumped heads, with Mr. Newton
B4 he started, his own personal using
Around the same time
B4 another legend would die
In the city of Los Angeles, Raymond Washington gave birth to the Crips
As a youth, he controlled the city, with a tight grip
Leather jackets, golf caps, guns, brass knuckles, and muscles behind fists
He ruled like a boss, but never had a chance to get rich
But, many men and women.
Have done many things, living through his influence and image
Like, Dr. Martin Luther King
This, man also had a dream
That all Crips would unite as one
And forever reign in his name, under the sun
Then, later on, came the Pirus and Bloods
Sylvester Scott and Vincent Owens,
Were known on the streets of Compton as thugs
Initiation and recruitment happened on Piru street
Outnumbered and outgunned, so they couldn't be weak
Although they'd put up a good fight, they were still viciously demolished
By their rivals, the "CC Ridas" their founder Mac Thomas
Whom now had resentment toward his old friend Raymond
For forming an alliance with the Pirus, he would forever now shame him
The Piru street family were now the Piru Crips
Nevertheless, by 1970 this all had shattered due to the constant conflict
As a result of this multiple Pirus sets had banded together
Joining forces with smaller groups like the Laurdes Park hustlers and the L.A brim's
Along with whoever!!!!
Would unite against the Crips
Under the one blood umbrella.

OUR STORY VS. HIS-STORY

Colored Regiments

Formed on September 21, 1966, at
Fort Leavenworth, Kansas
The nickname Buffalo Soldiers
Was adopted by Aboriginal men,
Recognized for their indigenous heritage.
Before then and during the civil war, the
United States had formed.
The United States Colored Troops regiments,
Which were composed of Aboriginal
Soldiers and Native Americans,
That only lasted a year.
Then the U.S.C.T. was officially disbanded,
Which most of the Buffalo Soldiers were U.S.C.T. veterans.
But as time went on,
Uncle Sam gradually decreased on.
Army units of all-Black regiments,
With much success, in the Indian wars;
Thirteen enlisted Buffalos and six of their officers.
Had earned the precious Medal of Honor.
Spending a year in New Mexico.
Pursuing the leader Victorio and his Apache warriors.
Ten years later, spending their winter,
guarding the Pine Ridge Reservation,
During the Ghost Dance War,
Removing Sooners from Native American
lands and not leaving until everything was restored.
Hardly recognized in his-story
Is the Buffalo Soldiers' participation in the
Johnson County War.
A conflict had erupted
Over the land in Wyoming,
that ended in gores.

When wealthy ranchers engaged, a band of hired killers.
They had a lengthy shootout, with not only local farmers.
But also a squad of sheriff posse hitters.
Enough was enough.
President Benjamin Harrison ordered in the 6th Calvary.
Their mission was to capture the hired killers and
bring peace through town meetings.
Unable to gain control and tame the situation,
The 9th Cavalry was specifically called on
To come in and be their replacement.
Although it took a year.
They had gotten Johnson County back in order.
Next up was the 1898 Spanish-American War.
Also included
Was the Battle of San Juan Hill on the island of Cuba.
Where five more Medals of Honor were earned by Buffalo Soldiers.
Celebrating, while doing the dance of Juba.
1899 to 1903.
Fighting for America again.
Only this time, it was in the Philippines.
While white soldiers broke out in cold sweats,
simultaneously commencing to vomit.
Colored men were nicknamed, yet again.
This time, being called the Immune Regiments.
Mistakenly believed to be resistant.
To all tropical diseases and elements.
Many brothas had begun establishing rapports with the
brown-skinned natives.
Most famously celebrated out of those troops
Was the legendary David Fagen.
Deserting their campaigns and joining the Filipino rebels,
Refusing to continue fighting in another war
On behalf of European devils.
But as for those who did continue to fight on;
Brought their new fight on to World War I.
The 10th Cavalry had fought at the Battle of Ambos Nogales.
Colored soldiers still had no sense of belonging,

While fighting in a white man's war for nationalism.
Assisting in the forced surrender of federal Mexican militia forces,
Buffalo Soldiers came through, riding on black horses.
Every ranking man was dressed in M1902 blues.
Then, on December 12, 1951,
The 27th and 28th Calvary units were the last to be discontinued.

Eclipse of Wealth

Today's nine richest men in the world
Has more wealth than the poorest four billion people on Earth.
After hearing that statistical fact,
Tell me it doesn't make you think about your own self-worth?
The wealthiest person ever to be recorded into this world history;
Net worth was an astounding $400 billion and he was the same
Pigmentation as me.
King Musa Keita.
Today better known as Mansa Musa.
Had inherited his empire by the default, Of his predecessor
sailing across the Atlantic.
Never to be seen again, last heading to Amaruka.
Abu bakr II had already appointed Musa deputy and chief
before he'd left.

Thoughts of a Convicted Felon

Although he wasn't of Royal blood.
The laws of their kingdom had made him that.
He would go on to rule for twenty-five years, as the emperor whom never lost a war.
Conquering over twenty-four cities and multiplying the Malinese empire like never before.
After coming into power, he paid tribute to his religious faith.
While not forcing his beliefs on any.
But fully establishing in his empire as a true Islamic State.
Founder of the first university ever to be erected in their region.
Timbuktu boasted of imported mathematicians, astronomers and Islamic professors that were worldly seasoned.
Pay was 200 kg of gold to build the Djinguereber mosque.
Workers were from southern Spain and all across the Muslim world.
All the while suffering from population decline by famine, the black plague and political revolution.
Was the entire continent of Europe.
While Africa, Amaruka and Asia were all hubs for trade, commercial and industry.
Mansa Musa took advantage of others economic instabilities.
Before his involvement with Timbuktu.
It had barely even been established, as a permanent place to settle.
But after his renovations.
Always coming through the city, were a constant stream of camels.
Confirming Timbuktu as the epicenter for commerce and trading.
He was also successful as a merchant, selling his gold all across Africa and Asia.
In a country wealthy in natural reserves.
Such as salt mines, gold mines and the perfect landscapes for farming.
Once inside the of the Mali empire.
It was considered to be a safe place all day, night and every morning.
Traders, travelers, visitors and citizens all lived peacefully together.
Because drastic measures would be taken on violent people and thieves.
Shown no mercy.
Chopping off hands, head's, torsos and knees.
Musa had turned Mali into one of the most important and largest Islamic African empires while still in his prime.

Also known throughout world history for conducting one of the most illustrious caravans of all time.
In the Muslim laws of the Quran.
It's mandatory.
That one must visit Mecca, at least once in a lifetime.
So for this trip.
The King has spared no expense.
Musa have provided all of the necessities.
Feeding the entire company of animals, slave women and men.
Rare foods and confectionery.
All would eat until one's need to stop was desired.
12,000 private slave women dressed in gowns of brocade and Yamanese silk for hire.
12,000 slave men each carrying 4 pounds of gold bars.
60,000 of his men all dressed in Persian silk and brocade.
Harold's bore gold staphs, organized horses and handled the bags.
80 camels carrying 50-300 pounds of gold dust.
In which to every poor person he passed.
Received enough gold dust to eventually crash.
The entire economy of Egypt for many years to come.
During his pilgrimage it was recorded that on every Friday.
Mansa Musa had built a Mass.
When Amanlik Amonsier had sent his messengers to summons Musa for a meeting.
At first the Mansa had tried to avoid this greeting.
Saying that he was merely passing through Cairo on his way to Mecca and had no business with their King.
When in actuality he didn't want to be a part of a ritual that was very insulting.
All in presence must bow down and kiss the Royal highness's feet.
The more messengers that continued to pursue.
He would continue to make, even more of an excuse.
The sultan had felt insulted and then demanded.
That Mansa Musa at once be brought, into his Royal presence.
The ball was in Amonsier's court and he had every bit of leverage.
Having no military to protect him from the thousands of slave warriors in attendance.

Musa had finally complied.
While conversations were based on diplomacy, religion and of course along business lines.
Ending with the two almost clashing.
Because Musa was too critical of Amonsier and far out swaggin.
After his pilgrimage to Mecca.
Many people around the world had heard how he spent his wealth freely and lived life lavish.
Eventually depicted in 1375.
On a world map called the Catalan Atlas.
But still and all.
The world's wealthiest man ever fortune had crumbled, after only two generations.
In less than 100 years.
His descendant spent recklessly and weren't as strategic in war-like situations.

Abolitionist
(The Raider and the Traitor)

May 4, 1800
Is when John Brown was born.
At Torrington, Connecticut.
But had spent most of his childhood in Hudson, Ohio on the family farm.
Devoutly religious as a youth.
He'd briefly studied for the ministries before quitting.
Deciding to follow in his Father's footsteps.
Because the Tanner's trade seemed to be a bit more fitting.
While on his mother's side of the family tree.
There was an unfortunate history of mental instability.
In which had eventually been passed down, through generations of genetic disabilities.
After marriage in 1820.
His wife had bore him seven children.

In which two of the bunch had suffered, from some sort of mental illness.
Then came the unfortunate and untimely death of the love of his life.
But John would remarry a year later.
Having even more children, with his newly found wife.
13 more.
To be of the exact.
Overall Brown had 20 children and 12 had survived out of his pack.
While at the tender age of 12.
John witness an event, that had forever changed his life.
The site of an Aboriginal boy, being beaten with a shovel.
By a grown white man, as the child begged for his life.
This had led Brown to declare eternal war.
Against all acts of slavery.
Later in this life concluding.
That it could only be abolished, by anointment in blood.
Ultimately through fine acts of bravery.
Deciding in 1839.
That South Africa should be invaded at gunpoint.
Freed of its slaves.
Then giveth land, diamonds, gold and the rights to run their own government.
Not only a revolutionary.
But John had tried his hand in a number of business ventures.
Failing at many of them and ending up in debt with debentures.
These events had caused him to move, his family at least 10 times.
Until came the year of 1849.
They'd found a settlement in North Elba, New York.
A private, project, financed on a farm known as Timbuktu.
Free Moors were being trained in arms like troops.
Around the same time came along, the Kansas-Nebraska act of 1854.
As territories hung and limbo between free and slave states.
This was his chance to jump into action of the revolutionary war.
Five of his sons headed onto Kansas, joining the free staters.
Sending him a call for help to their father a few months later.
Now traveling full of anger.
While gathering money for gun's.

He'd began to shout.
There could be "no remission of sin" in Kansas.
Without the shedding of blood."
Finally making it down to Kansas in mid-September.
He was here.
"The Great White hype of the niggers."
Settling himself near Osawatomie.
In his very own words, he said it's so grimy.
"I am here," "to promote the killing of slavery."
While leading a retaliatory raid.
He'd kill five men.
All in the name of anti-slavery.
In which he had been apprehended before escaping.
Oppositions on the other side, began to label him (insane) crazy.
But his son John Junior had to spend three months in jail as an accomplice.
He seemed to be on a roll and no one could stop him.
Now the Confederates had a target on his head.
Wanting very desperately, to kill him dead.
This event in Pottawatomie, had now made him nationally known.
But also caused him to become disowned.
By some of his own.
Frederick Douglass had declined joining Brown on many of his raids.
Thinking to himself that his good friend, was headed to an early grave.
Voicing to John Brown that it was only a suicide mission.
While Frederick Douglass was into fighting for freedom through written laws.
John Brown was on the front line and with the business.
Harriet Tubman had also refused his recourses.
Also wanting nothing to do with his raids.
So the topic wasn't up for discourses.
Spending the summer of 1856.
Collecting money for the war in Kansas.
From prominent public figures, in New England.
In which opportunity he'd taking full advantage.
Many of who were impressed by his dedication.
To the cause of abolition.

Thoughts of a Convicted Felon

Although some we're not wholly aware, of the exact details of his mission.
The Massachusetts Kansas Committee was on his side and they had his back.
Assisting with the gathering of recruits.
Also guns.
Along with money.
For future raids and attacks.
But during a battle that same year in August.
His son Frederick was killed.
Dying for what he believed in.
Fighting by his father's side, right on that Osawatomie field.
In early 1857.
John had gathered a group.
Out of Tabor, Iowa.
They marched fully trained and ready to shoot.
Now regularly holding meetings with Eastern abolitionists.
Has become the planting of seeds.
To bear fruit for the U.S. to one day witness.
Sending John Junior to surveillance the area around Harpers ferry in 1858.
Which was the site of a federal arsenal.
That John Senior had every intention to take.
All of their weapons and armor every slave in that state.
This was all discussed in a 10-day meeting.
Held in Chatham, Ontario, Canada for more than one reason.
That's where he left from to lead a raid.
Heading to Missouri under an alias, killing one man and freed some slaves.
In which he brought back to Canada with him.
Now brown was considered a criminal, not only by the state of Missouri.
But also every US government district.
While both sides had offered, handsome rewards for his capture.
He was still mostly known as a liberator in the North.
So donations had continued to poured in.
As he and his men would continue to gather.

By July of 1859.
John rented a farm five miles north of Harpers ferry.
Which is where 21 men were recruited, for one last final training.
16 were white and about 5 Aboriginals.
But on the night of October 16th 1859.
John rode to Harpers Ferry with 18 men and a wagon load of supplies.
Leaving three men just in case, to guard the farm behind.
After cutting the telegraph wire lines.
Brown and his men had slipped under the cover of darkness.
With ease capturing, the armories watchmen.
Allowing the midnight train to continue through, on its regular route.
But was spotted by a free Black railroad attendant, that tried warning the towns people.
As John Brown shot him dead in his boots.
Heyward Shepherd was the name of the traitor.
America even erected a small monument for him, as a national hero sometime later.
As shooting broke out between Brown's men and the Town's people.
Military soon arrived from Charles Town and now the situation had become unequal.
By the night fall.
Of that days end.
Trapped inside the armories engine house.
Was Brown and his men.
All were wounded.
With the exception of five.
Brown's son's Oliver & Watson.
Both were barely holding on to life.
The next morning 90 Marines had arrived.
They were dispatch for Washington.
Immediately storming into the engine house.
Slashing Brown severely with the tip of a sabre and bayonet along with two of his men.
7 were captured.
While death in the name of honor, had been the fate of 10.
John was jailed in Charles Town and then tried a week later.
Inside of the courtroom, lying wounded on a stretcher.

Refusing to move forward with their procedures and lectures.
But was more than ready, to endure his sentence.
So instead of putting up a defense.
He found it more pleasing, to just make an announcement.
"I believe that to have interfered as I have done."
"In behalf of his despised poor, I did no wrong, but right… I am ready for my fate."
The jury then indicted him, on three felony counts.
First degree murder, conspiracy with African Americans and treason against Virginia as a state.
The court had imposed the sentence of death by hanging.
John Brown was to be executed on November 2nd.
Which was only a month later.

Treasure, Genocide and Slavery in Haiti

In 1492 Columbus was the only one, that believe the Earth to be flat.
Ancient Egyptians chiseled hieroglyphs inside of pyramids and a circular shadow around the moon was cast.
Seafarers seen its roundness.
When ships would disappear, over the horizon.
Hull first, then the sail's above the Poseidon.
Just like the discovery of a new world, Christopher was given the credit.
In 1499 he made a major gold strike on Haiti.
Then forced hundreds of thousands of aboriginal's to mine or get beheaded.
A holocaust experiment.
Through so many attempts.
Soon came the taking of land, wealth and the transatlantic slave trade.
Trying to exterminate all of the indigenous people, a social underclass was made.
The Aboriginals in the Caribbean islands, welcomed Columbus with nothing but hospitality.
On the initial he was also friendly.
All while calculating thoughts, of heinous fatalities.
Less of a discover and more along the lines of a conqueror.
He kidnapped 25 Indians, captured parrots, stole gold trinkets and other exotica.
He then took them back, with him to Spain.
But only eight of his captives had survived.
There was quite a stir in Seville, once they have finally arrived.
Ferdinand and Isabella readily invested, giving funding for a second voyage.
Providing seventeen ships, 1500 men, attack dogs, crossbows, guns and cannons.
On the return mission to Haiti, in the year of 1493.
Columbus and his men demanded food, gold, spun cotton and whatever else they wanted or could see.
Including sex with their women and punishment by example.
Disfiguration for even a minor offense.

Thoughts of a Convicted Felon

To show that the Spaniards, were willing to trample.
The Spanish would cut off an Indians ear or nose brutally beyond humiliation.
Then send them back to their village, to ensure the rest cooperation.
After a while the Indians had, had enough and tried to rebel.
They refused to plant food for the Spanish and abandoned towns near settlements as well.
Finally the Aboriginals fought back with their only defense being sticks and stones.
They soon found out they were outmatched against the Spanish armed and clothed.
Their attempts at resistance, only gave Columbus an excuse to make war.
He set out to conquer the Aboriginals of Haiti.
In the year of 1495 March 24.
200 foot soldiers, 20 Calvary, with many crossbows, small cannons, lances and swords.
20 hunting dogs immediately tore Indians apart.
While Christopher enjoyed the sight on his horse from abroad.
Soldiers mowed down dozens with point blank volleys.
Dogs chase fleeing Indians into the brush, to rip open limbs and bellies of bodies.
Naturally the Spanish had won, with complete victory.
Killing many Indians and capturing others.
Whom were also made history.
After rounding up 1,500 Aboriginals, they selected the 500 best specimens to send to Spain.
Another 500 were also chosen by the Spanish, to stay on the island as slave's.
Spaniards hunted Indians for sport and murdered them for dog food.
Upset by not being able to locate gold, Columbus had set up a system of tribute.
Every three months, the Indians promised to pay homage.
In the Cibao, where the gold mines were, a large hawk's bell of gold dust went to the Catholic sovereigns.
A copper token about their necks was proof of making payment.
With a fresh coin he was safe, for another 3 months of slaving.

Any Indian found without such a token, was to be punished.
Those whose coins had expired, got a hand cut off just as a warning.
1502 is when Spain made the encomienda system, an official policy on Haitians.
Later other conquistadors introduce the same methods to Peru, Mexico and Florida Nations.
Colonists in Haiti even made the Indians, carry them everywhere they traveled.
Forcing natives to work in mines, rather than in their gardens.
This led to widespread malnutrition and sorrow.
Occasionally a hundred at a time, would commit mass suicide rituals.
Many women shunned childbirth and those pregnant aborted in intervals.
Some after delivery killed their children, at the mercy of their own hands.
Preventing from bringing them into such oppressive slavery, in a now curse land.
The intrusion of rabbits and other livestock, helped cause further ecological disasters.
But diseases new to the natives such as smallpox, had killed off Haiti's native populations with instanters.
Some tried fleeing to Cuba.
But the Spanish soon followed them there.
The "Black Legend" of Spanish cruelty, was on the island everywhere.
Christopher Columbus returned to Spain and left his brother Bartholomew in charge of the island.
A family tradition of accumulating wealth through slavery, genocide and violence.
Somewhere around 8 million Indian people inhabited Haiti, as a pre-Columbian estimation.
Bartholomew took a census of Indian adults in 1496 and came up with 1.1 million as the population.
Thanks to labor policies initiated by Christopher and the sinister slave trade.
By 1516 only some 12,000 natives remained.
In 1542 fewer than 200 Indians were alive, in the place they once called home.
By 1555, they all were gone???

The Last Discoverer

Three ships of death, set forth from Spain.
Heading towards and indigenous continent.
Where they'd spread many disease and its inhabitants would be enslaved.
After the year of 1493.
The Americas would never be the same.
Columbus is one of only two people, that the U.S. honors in a national holiday by name.
America's first great hero only the evil would say.
While aboriginal descendants, indigenous to these lands.
Of course feel a whole other way.
Hijacked, raped, robbed and pillaged.
Forced labor, convergence and genocides of village.
To be the first to find, learn of or observe.
The definition of discover.
Say's it all with simplicity, in those words.
I guess American his-story bypassed the Moors, China, Vikings and the Norse.

The only thing Christopher probably was first to do in America.
Was riding a pale white horse.
Ancient Egyptians and Phoenicians had already sailed, as far as England and Ireland.
Aborigines reached Australia, Polynesians arrived in Madagascar and Africans made it to the Canary Islands.
Columbus claimed everything he saw, right off the boat.
With subjugation on his mind, while gripping America's throat.
Ancient Roman coins with faces of Africanized features, keep turning up all over American land's.
Native Americans crossed the Atlantic a millennium ago, from Canada to (Scotland) Scottish-land.
Two Indians shipwrecked in Holland, around 60 BC.
Making Columbus's expedition not the first.
But more like the last discovery.
Curiosities of shores beyond Europe, led to an age of exploration.
European world domination and 500 years of exploitation.
The 1400's had ushered in an arms race, full of military technology advancements.
While other nations soon began to succumb falling prey.
Because of their disadvantage.
Europe was stirring with new ideas, in the Renaissance period.
A series of wars called the crusades, had caused great changes in their spirits.
The old trade routes to Asia, had always brought a difficult task.
People had grown more curious.
In search of better ways fast.
On a worldly level.
Most should agree that Columbus was behind schedule.
In 1005 the Vikings voyage to Vineland, their name for New England to settle.
There was contact between Norse and Indians around AD 1000.
Neither marked by domination.
But most encounters surely were violent.
Voyages of the Vikings having little lasting effects, on the fate of the world is simply transparent.
But daring Norse sailors.
Had reached America in intervals, journey after journey.

Crossing the North Atlantic, Iceland, The Farrow Island's, Baffin Land New Foundland, Labrador and New England.
The Norse settlement lasted for 500 years (982-c.1500), on the continent of Greenland.
That's just as long as in U.S. European settlement.
In the America's, up to date.
An 800 year rule came, even before that race.
Expeditions were launched from Morocco.
But ultimately from Egypt.
In the gulf Coast lands of Mexico.
Is where Africans and indigenous Amurakans have breeded.
The rise of Olmecs came, in 100 to 750 BC.
Afro Phoenicians set the standard for the earliest multiracial societies.
Unlike the Norse.
Africans made a permanent impact on the America's.
All before Columbus was even born.
So who discovered, what?
Realistic portraits of West Africans, chiseled into stone head structures.
Organic colossal heads of basalt, stood along the eastern coast of Mexico ruptures.
Enormous effort was taken to quarry, the sculpt into heads ten feet tall from rocks.
Carved Negroid facial expressions, to be remembered forever.
The human models Olmec heads, come from a people so clever.
Important people to be worshiped, or at least obeyed.
Negro American ancestry, consist of more than just slaves.
The Portuguese explorer Vasco da Gama, sailed around Africa in 1497.
Africans beat the gamma more than 2,000 years and we're already experts at navigation and selling.
When Columbus reached Haiti, Africans were already there.
He'd found Aboriginals in possession of guanine.
An alloy identical to gold, that the Africans prefer to wear.
Traces of diseases common in Africa, have been detected in pre-Columbian corpse of Brazil.
Columbus's son Ferdinand had made contact with Africans, in Eastern Honduran fields.
The first European to reach Panama, reported seeing Black slaves in an Asiatic Indian Town.

The natives said they had captured them, from a Black community a few miles down.
No one seems to know Columbus social class upbringing, or where he really comes from.
He claimed to be from Italy.
But didn't seem able to write in Italian at all.
Some said he grew up lower class, the son of a poor Genovese weaver.
Others insist he came from wealth, the son of a prosperous wool weaver.
One thing's for sure.
To be a discover, he sure had a lot of predecessors.
So how did the last discover.
Become the prime successor?
Well I guess if the discoverer wasn't white.
Then it never was found.
Europeans rule the world and everyone else must bow.

California Queen

Reigning over the empire of the Xi, was the queen of gold and diamonds.
A decorated warrior, mother, strategic opponent and also your Royal Highness.
Of a people who were trainers and lovers of exotic animals indigenous to their lands.
These ancient indigenous Californians domesticated snakes, eagles, tigers, bears and Griffins.
Maintained cultural communication and trading contacts.
With Africa, Australia and those along the South Pacific.
A territory spanning many thousands of miles throughout California.
From the coast of San Francisco.
To Baja Mexico.
Every Pacific islander Nation.
Including Hawaii, Australia, Fiji, Tonga and Samoa.
In which all of these lands and islands.
A great warrior Queen named Khalifa had once ruled over.
Known for their long dark flowing hair, robust bodies and Black skin.
As well as inhabitants of her state, were all of the same descent.
Highly sophisticated scientist, priest and mathematicians.
Music enthusiast performing arts and nautical wizards.
Worshippers of Egyptian gods like Horus, Osiris, Isis, Maat and Ra.
While tracking the celestial Sirius star system abroad.
Over 100,000 cave paintings, ancient artifacts and symbols.
" In Living Color " worship of their gods, snakes, crosses, marriage ceremonies, scuba mask, gold mining, electricity and guns.
Along with many other things resembled.
Africans have been "Coming to America"
Before slavery, before Columbus and thousands of years before Christ.
Moors and other indigenous nations had already established thriving civilizations in ancient "Amurakaan" times.
100,000 years ago if you like me to be more precise or even exact.

Queen Califia and the California Blacks of California…
Were descendants of the Olmecs, Egyptians, Kings of Kush, West African Mending and the first emperor of China (Shandi's, Shang Dynasty) are all archaeological facts.

STOLENLEGACY

How could one be so evil?
For these people have stolen artifacts from our history and turn them into world museums.
Stole our dreams and produced to U.S. nightmares.
Charging the descendants of ancestral emperors, Kings, prince's, princesses and Queens Euros to visit their tombs.
Ancient tribal rivalries of West Africa, had helped enslave their own kind.
In which eventually led to the continents doom.
Napoleon Bonaparte had proclaimed himself a conqueror.
But, couldn't win one war.
Shot noses off of sphynx and stole the Rosetta Stone for scores.
The key to ancient Egyptian writings, had been stolen by pale faced pleasantly thrives.
It was written in the three scripts of hieroglyphs, demotic and Greek.
They worked hard to decode our language and discovered what it means to be Kings.
Secrets of the throne, transfers of energy and trips to other realms.
Our dear Rosetta Stone had ended up in British hands.
Whom were the victors, that ran Napoleon and his army out of African land's.
After the Brit's were done raping Egyptian tombs, pyramids and cities.
Egypt was then handed down to the Turks.
Whom were very eager to trade and gain technology.
Immediately, they went to work.
Foreigners were now encouraged to come to Egypt, for archaeology was now a diplomatic tool.
Powerful visitors with exotic hobbies.
Flooded the Nile, in search of quick fortune and rule.

Free Bodies of Lost Tribes

Free at last.
The slaves, would shout aloud.
Without a plan.
Nor a roof overhead.
Or even a bed.
No home to come upon, for a sense of pride.
Only recent memories of lynchings and other gruesome ways so many of our people had died.
Everyone is looking lost, searching for a sense of direction.
Many would stay in the south, while others began " The great migration."
I have to start another family.
Because, I was separated from my wife.
My children.
I'd probably, wouldn't even notice.
And, out of my parents children I was the oldest.
Not to mention, that at the tender age of five.
Our father.
Was tied by his four limbs to horses and torn apart right before our eyes.
I've been through so much pain in my life.
That when I die.
I probably would feel it twice.

Crosses

Christians in Spain were having trouble finding common grounds and suffering from a lack of unity.
At this time alliances between Muslims and Christians states, were a common practice in many Spanish communities.
Due to this matter most of the Iberian peninsula had been conquered, by Muslims from Morocco along the northern African Coast.
The Cordoba caliphate once governed by Visigoths, for the next four hundred years would be under Moorish rule and control.
None of these events have sat well with the more advanced Christian kingdoms, that were located further north of Spain.
Muslims now control most of their country, but Christians had managed to survive five of their northernmost States.
Catalonia, Aragon, Castile and Leon.
All the while Portugal received heavenly rewards, for gaining independence of there now prospective throne.
Finally strong enough to make an attempt, at retaking many of their lost territories.
The reconquista had just begun with the uniting of once sworn enemies, who all discovered at heart a similar glory.
Now, with the backing of Pope Urban II great benefits would be afforded.
Religion could be used as a tool and contributions to the church was really extortion.
Bearing crosses, marching down the battlefield, with offerings of mass preaching in order to gain more recruits.
Raising of church taxes to fund their armies, along with promises of going to heaven, in which all had known the Reverend had a direct route.
Hired arms and assassins were also imported to assist in the fight, of this now so called holy war.
2 military orders of professional warrior monks, whom were called knights Hospitaller and the Knights Templar.

Whom to which Alfonso I of Aragon had given large portions, of his very own estate having no hoarder.

In avoidance of sending contributions to the Middle East, caused many kingdoms to form their own local knighthood orders.

These acts of heroism had launched a new type of spirit, that now spread all throughout the Iberian peninsula.

Now other European rulers would help in the aid, of saving the land of their fellow Christian familia.

Which this was most important to Norman, Sicily.

Whom had been the Moors, long ago sworn enemies.

The first victory would be in 1212, at Las navas de tolosa.

A blow dealt by three Spanish Christian kingdoms, that the Spanish Muslims would never recover from.

Then came a series of furthermore gains, such as the recapture of Valencia and Cordoba within two years apart.

10 years later they would retake the Seville, leaving heavily fortified Granada as the one and only last standing Muslim blocks.

Some of the Spanish Moors converted into Christianity and were now known throughout Spain as Moriscos.

Many Christians were then encouraged to move southward, replacing Arab names off buildings and even their mosque had conversion potentials.

Of course this all would come to an end, when ushered in the year 1492.

The Spanish Crown was no match for North African soil, so the conquest of small islands would have to do.

Their mission into the new-old-world, was to spread Christianity through acts of violence.

But they were wolves in sheep's clothing, with their real intentions on first contact always disguised in silence.

With this came acts of genocide, rape, manipulation, segregation and plenty of class play rehearsals.

Mis-educational conditioning by foreign Invaders, telling his-story in the form of reversal.

Before the Nina, pinta, or Santa Maria had ever arrive at any island or Amarukaan shores.

Christopher Columbus knew exactly where he was headed because he was expertly navigated by berbers and Moors.
Although now finally liberated were the Christians of Spain.
Now an Omen had been placed on Aboriginal natives of Turtle Island, whom were now cursed 400 years physically and mentally enslaved.
Ever since then indigenous peoples, have been lied to about our origins.
From adolescent years, on to adulthood, our brains are instilled with poisons.
Michael Jackson said don't believe their lies!!!
American his-story books, they're all filled with lies!!!
Our teachers
Teach U.S.
That we all came to Amaruka, from Africa on ships as slaves.
When it's obvious we're the real Indegenous Americans, the same place where our ancestors lay.

Born and Raised in Captivity
(Life of a Stud)

As violent waves of the Atlantic, continued to beat across the bottom of the ship's exterior.
While riding high tides the precious cargo of slaves, rode beneath the decks of its interior.
A birth and a death had happened, on this very same voyage.
It was somewhere around the year of 1810, when these events all unfolded.
Mary was a captured teenager, whom originated from Ghana.
Due to tactics of rape and abuse, a man of prominence from Hazing, England by the name of John William Heath was now the father.
Of a newborn baby boy born into slavery, by the way whose name was William Heath Sr.
Soon after the birth of her son, Mary had become very ill and her body produced a fever.
The other West Africans did everything they could in their power, through many attempts of trying to save her life.
She had eventually fell into a state of an eternal slumber, before forever saying good night.
JW Heath then ordered the body of the infant child's mother, to be thrown overboard the ship.
Her body then sank into a watery grave, being swallowed by the oceans abyss.
Already born to the beyond harsh, circumstances of slavery.
But, now without a mother to console and nurture him nor a designated person to care for this baby.
The ship's course ended at the shores, of an island in the Grand Bahamas.
Here's where the baby was purchased, by a female plantation owner of many slaves, for only a small sum of dollars.
William had grown up to be a dark brown skin large and very strong boy in the early years of his teens.

Also becoming uncontrollable by the male plantation owner, whose own mistress has spoiled him it seemed.
He was then sold off to another, but at this time still resided in the Bahamas.
This is where his personality had grown to become somewhat darker.
Mean and hateful just like a bull.
His new owner used him as a stud slave, for the cost efficient purposes of a male breeding tool.
Unable to get along with anybody, but well worth his weight in gold.
On, November 5th of 1865.
William Heath Sr was shackled, blindfolded and once again sold.
This time he was marched to the ramp of a ship, owned by his new owner.
Which later landed in Virginia, where many more deals for his body will continue to be brokered.
Finding himself to be sold from this plantation, then to that plantation and rented on others.
Continuously raped of his seed.
Williams body had no longer belonged to him, any more than his impregnated lovers.
Tight curly hair, dark smooth skin and large in stature.
Known for causing trouble amongst the other slaves, doing whatever he wanted and accepting the punishments that would surely come to him thereafter.
From sun up to sundown.
William would work the tobacco fields hostile, angry and bitter.
Often used as a stallion to mate, he took it upon himself to rape and procreate slave women.
Once again finding himself being sold, to the highest bidder.
Never being able to settle and live a stable life.
Until he eventually married a woman by the name of Sarah Drummond, giving her his last name and the title of being his wife.

Greenwood Massacre (1921)

At a time when the state of Oklahoma only had two airports, six wealthy Black families owned all of their planes.
Coming from a sophisticated all Black community that boasted of owning their own Banks, hotels, movie theaters, clothiers, contemporary homes and many cafes.
Even the luxuries of indoor plumbing, along with a superior school system.
Rather than having a traditional American education, which still today our peoples are a victims.
Undoubtedly they were highly resented, by their less-fortunate white neighbors.
They were surrounded by upper class Blacks, that had surpassed their enslavers.
Full of cruel intentions and they're jealous desires.
The plan was to put high achieving copper-colored peoples in their place, and then set their town on fire.
In a wave of domestic white terrorism and suppression.
In order to remain Master's, they cost black dispossession.
This once powerful community was known as, the Black Wall Street on a national scale.
It all started back in 1906.
O.W. Gurley an African American man from Arkansas, whom moved to Tulsa purchasing 40 acres of land, to which of whom only other African American men that he would sell.
Gurley now provided opportunity, for those migrating from the harsher place of Mississippi.
Colored families average income in the area, exceed what minimum wage is today in the 21st century.
It's rumored that a dollar, would have circulated 36 to a hundred times. And would remain in greenwood, for at least a year before saying goodbye.

But, still their economic status couldn't save them, from the racial hostility of their day.
The area had been bombed by, US government fighter planes.
But, the "Tulsa Race Riots" is what the papers would say.
Nitroglycerin and kerosene had caused, the inferno to blaze most aggressively.
Neither the survivors, nor their families received the reparations of their equity.

El Yanga
(San Lorenzo De Los Negros)

Lacking the knowledge of superior technology, was a great way to become targeted and enslaved.
Time and time again throughout world history, it probably happened to every last race.
Some enslaved their own.
But, most had admired the physics of the darker-skinned people's.
Because in comparison to any other, there could be no equals.
When this happened to Gasper Yanga, he decided to fight back.
Due to his heroic acts, at least one town in Mexico had still remained Black.
Managing to rebelled against his captors, as well as being granted land.
All of this from an African escaped slave, in the "land of no pity", of no man's land.
Renegade communities had been established and were now being recognized all over New Spain.
These Palenques were all spread across Mexico's gulf Coast and now they're living status had changed.
At this time captive Africans, were not only good for agricultural labor.
They were also indispensable to these European foreigners, because their potentials were far more greater.
Brazil would be said to only come second to New Spain, which had the highest of all in enslaved populations.
But, of course many other countries had these same types of camps for their very own concentration.
The very same slaves that would be responsible, for building most of today's great Nations.
By 1576 the entire Veracruz coast region, had begun to see Palenques of indigenous Black people and runaway slaves.
Palenque life were far more simpler than any of them were used to, but far more Superior to escaping their graves.
Sustenance farming was a must.

So that to ensure all would remain, in high spirits along with good health.
Religion was heavily African featured.
But, still left room for indigenous beliefs as well.
Any Spaniard who dared, to travel Mexico's Camino Real.
Had to be suicidal and we're most definitely killed.
Anytime the "Spanish Crown" would joy ride "The Royal Road", their caravans would be robbed.
Forget about Robin Hood men in tights, beware of these aboriginal peoples who were really on their job.
Palenque camps were hidden deep in the woods, of the coastal Highlands.
On-site, all merchants and military alike.
Would suffer a violent death produced by crude weaponry, on no man's island.
For over three decades Spain would remain, unable to rein in the resistance.
Mostly due to the Gabonese Prince N'Yanga, whom was full of so much vigilance.
A man that refused to be, any other man's slave.
Coming from Central African royalty, he would rather die inside of a shallow grave.
In 1570, he made his great escape from Nuestra Senora de la Concepcion plantation.
Where he and members of his once Royal Court had killed 23 Spaniards and that had become the beginning of the Mexican Gabon Nation.
The Spanish Crown could never beat Yanga, although they surely tried.
Battle after battle along the shores of the coast, many Spaniards had died.
By 1609 The colony government of what's today they called Mexico, have been forced to take action.
The Spanish King Charles V. of old Spain had wrote a letter to New Spain stating.
The way this "Moor" is disrespecting "The Crown" is very unattractive.
"If you don't stop him, surely more slaves will follow."
Some 550 troops were immediately assembled, in the name of Spain.

All whom had marched out of Puebla, gunning for Yanga at full throttle.
Countering them with 400 men armed with crude weaponry, bow and arrows, rocks and freshly sharpened machete's.
Masters of their lay of land, along with 100 Gunners were the Palenque's.
Prince Yanga now attempted to broker a treaty, but the Spanish had refused to acknowledge his terms.
This resulted in a historic bloody battle, in which at the end of, a primary yanga settlement would be burned.
As rebels scurried into the mountains, and headed over the hills.
A victory this day could not be named, only just to keep it real.
But at the end of the day, the Yanga settlement had come back together.
Then in 1632.
New Spain had come to an conclusion, that would have never happened in the Northern part of America.
The Viceroy Rodrigo Pacheco had negotiated, with the now age Veracruz ruler.
The Palenque's agreed to no longer enticed slaves and the Yanga followers would own their land.
This sat very well with "El Yanga", although this left them with no more room to expand.

Fight for Power

The Black panther party was formed in October of 1966, in an act of self-defense.
Against racist pale faced cops, that patrolled Aboriginal communities back then.
Their goals were set on reaching the establishment of real economics for their people, along with political equality and social acceptance.
Huey P Newton and Bobby Seale together had founded this organization, that were also known for outlandishly in public carry their weapons.
Dressed in all black from head to toe.
Amoorican communities across the country, would for the first time in his-story have their own local militant presence.
Which eventually not only upset the local police departments, but also caught the attention of the U.S. president.
The first issue of the Black panther paper, went into distribution on April 25th of 1967.
When came the following month.
The party had marched on the California state capitol fully armed, but this time their pictures were taken by oppositional pressmen.
There to protest the state's attempt at outlawing, the carry of loaded firearms in public.
Then as Bobby Seale read a statement of protest from a bullhorn.
The police arrested him and all 30 armed Panthers and just like that their plans were immediately interrupted.
Through this early act of political repression.
The party ignited a flame across the states and soon formed other party chapters Nationwide in their fight against oppression.
Then came bad news for Huey Newton, in October of 1967.
He was arrested and accused for the heinous crime, of sending an Oakland cop to heaven.
Eldridge cleaver was then appointed by the organization to replace Mr. Newton, as defense minister upon the ranks of the militant structure.

The first thing he did was form a United movement, in order to free their brother.
Their devotion to "free Huey" in coming years, would take a lot of energy and need a great deal of attention.
All the while furthermore spreading their roots into political spectrums, working with various revolutionary parties and forming new coalitions.
Through the party's interactions with a group called, The Student Non-violent Co-ordinating Community (SNCC) many bonds were sealed.
In February of 1968 one of their recruits named Stokely Carmichael, became the Panthers prime minister over the field.
Carmichael was adamantly against whites, joining the movement of the Black liberation.
Explaining that they could never relate to our people's struggle and would only come with their own ideas of change through manipulation.

Black Caesar

If there ever were a true "American Gangster,"
I guess they forgot to make a movie about him.
I can't stand when at the end of every episode,
Them niggas turned snitch.
How the fuck did all of these rats gain the glory?
Well not this time
Because I'm about to give you a real one's story.
Born on February 13 in the year of 1944,
Frank Larry Matthews, a real "American Gangster" was born
In Durham, North Carolina, most likely on a farm.
His mother had died
When he was only the tender age of four.
"Pee Wee" had become his childhood nickname and he dropped out of school in the seventh grade.
Then by the age of fourteen,
He was running his own teenage gang;
They would steal chickens from every local farm
Until one day, Matthews was caught by a
Farmer and received a full assault.
In this event, he had been hit over the head with a brick.
They charged him with theft and he served a year for that shit.
Raleigh State Reformatory for Boys.
Once released, he moved to Philadelphia.
That's where he began working the numbers game for scores.
He made connections that would later become his future drug contacts.
Major Coxson and the Black Mafia had all of the cities respect.
After his arrest in 1963,
Frank avoided conviction by agreeing to leave.
So, Matthews moved to the Bedford-Stuyvesant area of New York City,
Becoming a barber and collecting numbers as he did in Philly.
After his years as an enforcer,
He just became
Tired of the same old numbers game,

Transitioning himself straight into the heroin drug trade.
The plan was to make more money and have it his way.
In the early 1960s,
The main wholesale supplier of heroin was the Italian mafia.
Through their "French Connection,"
They controlled the drug trade and there was no stopping them.
That's until both the Gambino and Bonanno crime families.
Had turned Frank down on his proposition.
But he wasn't shit out of luck
Because from his days in the numbers game,
He had his "Spanish Connections."
"Spanish Raymond," a numbers runner,
Introduced Frank to "El Padrino."
The New York Cuban Mafia godfather had that A-1 perico.
When they'd met it had been all perfect timing.
Very soon after "El Padrino" fled to Venezuela,
In order to avoid an drug indictment,
For $20,000, Matthews bought his first kilo from "El Padrino.,
Promising to supply more in the future to his new amigo.
Their relationship expanded and became very lucrative.
Receiving large loads of cocaine and heroin from South America
Was how Frank Matthews made his first millions.
All within a year,
He became one of the major players inside the New York drug business.
Never sticking to only one plug;
Continually seeking out new sources for drugs.
Frank would do business with anyone,
As long as the product was pure.
He had developed a cocaine habit
That grew along with his money and power.
By the early 1970s,
The Matthews Organization was distributing
Multimillion-dollar loads of powder.
Estimated by the IRS to have made $10 million dollars in 1972
From controlling the cutting, packaging and sales of heroin
In every major city on the entire East Coast.
In Brooklyn, Frank operated two massive drug mills,

Which were heavily fortified and secured.
Walls were reinforced with concrete and steel.
Protected by guards, with machine guns, on the roofs.
Suppying other major dealers throughout the United States with birds.
Minus the coops.
Frank purchased a mansion on Todt Hill, Staten Island,
Which was a known Mafia enclave.
Right across the street from him,
Lived Mafia crime boss, Paul Castellano.
In Philadelphia, he would supply his business friend, Major Coxson,
Whom would, in return, make his profits off of the Black Mafia.
Taking multiple trips, with suitcases full of cash to Viva Las Vegas.
Matthews laundered his drug money at casinos for a fee of 15 to 18%.
In 1971,
Matthew's invited every Hispanic and Copper-Colored
Drug trafficker in the country to a meeting.
As fancy high-end vehicles lined the block,
Drug Enforcement agents' gazes were entreating.
The topic discussed
Was how to import heroin without the Mafia,
Deciding to build stronger independent bonds with
The Cubans and those from Corsica.
Also agreeing to incorporate more cocaine in the game.
Mostly because it was more readily available through their drug chain.
This meeting had indeed changed the
Nature of the United States drug business.
Now other nationalities had established their own pipelines,
As the mob could only eyewitness.
Black drug dealers had begun taking over their own communities.
Local gangs began eliminating out of town suppliers and
Got in on the opportunity.
On Easter Sunday of 1972 in Atlantic City,
The Matthews Organization and the Black Mafia's business
Relationship had come to ends, finally.
Black Mafia members had killed Tyrone "Mr. Millionaire" Palmer,
Who was Matthews' main dealer in Philadelphia and it all
Went down at "Club Harlem."

Six hundred people had attended this club that night,
In which many innocent bystanders had been shot.
During the gunfight
Five people murdered and another twenty-six were injured.
When none of the seven hundred ninety-nine
Potential witnesses had come forward,
The shooters had escaped the justice system unhindered.
Three of Matthews' top lieutenants in the city were also murdered.
Contracts were issued and bodies were left hanging from girders.
But the game don't stop and the show must go on.
Frank hosted another drug dealer summit.
This time in Las Vegas at the Sands Hotel and
Muhammad Ali performed.
Authority was soon given for the police to tap his phones.
That's when Matthews was recorded discussing drug transactions and
His cover was blown.
Charged in Skengfield, Florida, for attempting to sell forty
Pounds of cain.
Then in January of 1973,
The DEA charged him in Las Vegas for conspiracy to distribute
Heroin and tax evasion.
Originally, his bail was set at $5 million,
Which was the highest bail amount ever set at the time.
Eventually being reduced to $2.5.
Only after Matthews had agreed not to fight his New York extradition.
His bail was again reduced to $325,000
After only a few weeks sitting in the New York detention.
Six counts of tax evasion and multiple drug conspiracy charges
Had him now facing fifty years in prison.
On July 2, 1973,
Frank Matthews was scheduled to appear in federal court in Brooklyn.
Not showing his face in the United States ever again.
Allegedly taking $20 million dollars in cash, he fled the
Country with his girlfriend.
Leaving behind his common-law wife and three sons.
To live in their Staten Island Mansion and was never seen again.
Not even by them.

Aztec Evolution

(1150) An empire that once spread through most of Central Mexico and had began to crumble.
Long periods of drought's and internal factional conflicts that ended in rumbles.
During the civil war, their city was burned and looted.
Rumors went around about how the Chichimec wild tribes of the North, would be the only ones bold enough to do it.
As the Toltec empire, had come upon its end.
(1200) Rival city-states battled for power, over the secession of their lands.
Around 1248 was the induction of Aztecs, into the Mexican Valley. Armed with key organizational and ideological principles adopted from Toltec refugees through their passing.
In 1300, the Aztec's were still just a miniature tribe.
Vagrants in search of a permanent territory in which they could reside.

All of the good lands were already occupied, by the more established nation's.
But, what insured their survival, was besides being fierce warrior's, they were also experts at cultivation.

Aztec Revolution

Inspired by their war God "Hummingbird on the Left".
They offered their services as mercenaries, to the locals that they just met.
But, often their barbarous behavior's offended most of the Kings.
How they would capture local women and make them their Queen's.
While working for the people of Colhuacan, the Aztecs obtained a princess.
Asking for the noble bride, for them was good for business.
In regards of the Aztecs, showing their token of appreciation.
Their priest had donned her skin, after the mutilation.
The Colhuacan were so angered, after such an event.
Immediately drawing weapons and then killing many of them.
Now, completely driven and forced out of their new-found land.
The site of an eagle perched onto a cactus, was a sign that they should form a new home on this nearby island.
It was this very same place, where Tenochitlan is located today.
Eventually the Aztecs formed an alliance with neighbors inland.
Then began their expansion of conquering rival tribes and their entire city-states.
Through this consortium, they had benefited greatly.
By learning teachings that the Tepanecs had used to build their own empire and the Aztecs even Incorporated a Navy.
But, soon after the passing of the old Tepanec ruler.
His son and successor's until then hidden jealousy, had grew even more.
Concerned, that their allies had grown too strong under their protection.
The Aztecs had found themselves once again, in this new land forced to draw their weapons.
Under the leadership of a brilliant military strategist, within a year they had crush their rivals.

Mercy of Ba'al

Born in a war-torn city, in the year of 247 BCE.
After Rome's victory in the first Punic war, they had stripped Carthage of his most important province.
Sicily…
Carthage had been the Mediterraneans most important seaport and also possessed other wealthy territories along the coast.
But, when civil war had broken out in the city.
Rome seized Sardinia and Corsica, this time concluding in the loss of a double dose.
These dreadful blows to his City surely, had made a great impression on the young Hannibal.
Whom, was the eldest and most skillful son of a Carthaginian general.
At the age of 10 years old, his father took him on a trip to Iberia.
A place where several Carthaginian cities laid among the Andalusia interior.
"Castle-Cadiz", "Royal Town"-Malaga, New Carthage, Cordoba and "Kart Town".
All were new lands added to his informal empire, in order to compensate for overseas territories that were lost now.
This is where his father made him promise, to forever possess internal hatred towards the Romans.
After his father's death in 229, Hannibal vowed to never forget the late generals Omen.
His son-in-law whom was a politician, took over command of the kingdom.
The new governor surely had proved himself to be, full of that Carthaginian wisdom.
Furthermore by improving their position by diplomatic means.
Intermarriage with Iberians, had become a regular theme.
Hannibal had eventually married a princess solidifying the bond.
Often visiting Carthage the land which he was born.
In 221, the nobleman had been murdered.

Hannibal was then elected to command and govern.
Exercising his father's old aggressive military tactics in politics.
He attacked the natives, capturing Salamanca at the age of 26.
Within a year he besieged Saguntum, whom were Roman allies.
At this time Rome was busy in their second Punic war, with those Lyrian guys.
This made them to be unable, to support the town.
In which resulted to Carthage, making them bow down.
Unbeknownst to the young general, this act had been a violation of previous treaties.
The Roman republic felt offended and demanded Hannibal be extradited immediately.
As negotiations about his fate went on, due to furthermore discussion.
He continued extending his territory and appointed commander of the Iberian government to one of his brothers.
In May 218, Hannibal had crossed the river Ebro.
Upon hearing this news, Rome declared the second Punic war and it was about to get medieval.
Immediately sending reinforcements to Sicily, where they expected their rivals would attack.
Instead the general had interrupted his campaigns in Catalonia and decided a bold invasion of Italy was more suitable than that.
37 elephants 9000 Calvary and 50,000 infantry.
Armed to the teeth as they cross the Pyrenees.
Then ferried his elephants, across the river Rhone on large rafts.
Not to mention his heroic efforts, do the coming down of heavy snow that Autumn attracts.
The most horrendous part of their journeys was crossing the Alps.
It had taken the Romans many years to figure that route.
October 218, 8,000 Calvary and 38,000 soldiers had crossed the plains.
Alongside the River Po, in an Italian town called Turin.
Which was inhabited by Gauls, whom had by Rome recently been subjected.
They welcomed Hannibal and his men in arms, with open arms and their mission was well respected.
His courage and enticement had hyped the Gauls into rebellion.
Their first engagement took place, at the River Ticinus East of Turin.

This had become an act of victory, together over their opponents.
Immediately some 14,000 Gauls had volunteered to serve under the general and help continue the wrath of his father's Omen.
Successful in a second battle, at the River of Trebia.
Which today would be west of modern Piacenza.
Then came the early spring of 217.
After leaving his winter quarters at Bolonia, he traveled the Apennines and ravaged Etruria.
Losing an eye in a minor separate engagement, but some historians claim he suffered from Opthalmia.
The Romans Consul had planned a counterattack with some 25,000 men.
But were defeated in an ambush between a Lake and some hills, dying at the "Mercy of Ba'al" in the hands of Hannibal and his men.
Now somewhat cocky after the defeat of two Roman legions.
He expected his rivals allies to cut ties and leave them.
However, this was not the case and his assumption was never complied.
So he gathered his multitude and crossed the Apennines one more time.
Hoping to establish a new base on the "Heel of Italy".
Meanwhile, Rome was attacking his lines of communication and supply base in Iberia where they killed many.
While Hannibal tried winning over their allies by diplomatic means.
The Romans appointed Fabius Maximus on their behalf, a magistrate with extraordinary powers and there to intervene.
But, all he did was tail the invader and then evaded the battle.
For evermore being marked down in Roman history, as a coward that skedaddled.
Then came in the year, of 216.
The Roman senate decided it were time for one great conclusive fight, in order to settle this thing.
No risk would be taken the consuls raised an army of nothing short of 80,000 soldiers.
While Hannibal's army accounted for 50,000 warriors or less to hold them over.
On July 6th in the neighborhood of Cannae on the Italian East Coast...

The Romans had the Carthaginian army stuck between a rock and a hard place fa'sho!!
The battle was ignited in August, enough was enough and it was no more time for play.
As the Roman elite troops fortified their structure towards the center. Hannibal's convex crescent-shaped infantry lines, slowly had became concaved.
This is when the Carthaginian Calvary in the rear, began encircling the Romans leaving them no room to divert the more clever.
Failing to break through enemy lines, they were mutilated destroyed and severed.
Another victory over the Romans, had brought Hannibal and his men so much joy.
After this event many of their adversaries supporters, were now quick to switch side's rather then also be destroyed.
The Sardinia revolt made it possible for Capua to become Hannibal's capital in Italy.
At 30 years old he entered Capua, parading on his last surviving elephant all throughout the city.
His brother Mago Barca, was then sent back to Carthage.
Announcing the great news in person, of the conquest ending triumphant.
The entrance of the Carthaginian Senate building.
Was the destination he'd chosen to pour out hundreds of golden rings, taken off of the bodies of Roman soldiers after they killed them.
However, the Senate refused to come to terms and Rome's closest counterparts in Central Italy have remained loyal.
Hannibal's plan now was to dissipate the Roman strength and make them coil.
Yet another shot at a more diplomatic approach, was launched by him in the early winter of 215.
This time he secured an alliance with Philip V, the late Macedonian King.
In 214, Syracuse had become an Carthaginian ally as well.
From the looks of things, general Hannibal's plan could only prevail.
As we all know, nothing lasts forever.

Meanwhile Rome had regained self-confidence and began thinking a little more clever.
Hannibal attempted to capture necessary Ports, that were needed in order to receive fresh troops.
Failing to do so successfully, led him back to the drawing board constructing a plan and regroup.
Coming to the realization, of possibly meeting his fate.
Deciding to abandon his sights in central Italy, if he wanted to see out his days.
Now, he directed his attention towards the southern Italy division.
This is where he would in 213, capture Tarentum as well as several other Port provinces.
Now fully able to facilitate supplies coming in, along with the wealth of soldiers.
They then had flooded the harbors, with ships from Carthage and Macedonia.
Rome countered this action, by an alliance in Aetolia which was Greek Town.
This caused the Aetolian League to start a war against Macedonia, so Hannibal fortified more of his troops down.
Also, sending an reinforcement on to Sicily.
But, the general himself did not receive too many.
In 212, Rome was back thinking on the initiative.
Cutting off Hannibal's lines of contact, was their game plan repetitive.
First they sent super armies, on to recapture Syracuse and Capua.
Syracuse had been betrayed to Marcellus and re-entered the Roman alliance in this ongoing duel.
In the mist of the fight, a famous scientist named Archimedes of Syracuse had been killed.
The Roman siege of Capua had lasted long, but in the end they failed.
Hannibal realized that his exhausted troops, would not be able to hold this position.
Exercising a diversionary attack on the city of Rome, was now his new mission.
This plan had failed, to no avail.
Because the Romans knew their City could not be swept.
So, the siege on Capua had continued with much success.

Then in 211, it was once again a Roman province.
Pressure being put on to the general's forces, had pushed them further more South of the matter.
To make situations even worse, in 209 the city Tarentum had been recaptured.
Now, his own government was unwilling to risk the sending of any more extra troops.
The lines of contact were too long, but Hannibal still be refused to withdraw and would never subdue.
So, he reached out to his brother Hasdrubal, whom were still in charge of Iberian armies.
But, now Carthaginians crossing the Alps.
To the Romans, was no longer alarming!!!
Due to this Hasdrubal was defeated at the River of Metairie, before he could even reach his brother.
Hannibal's hope of reinforcements now, had become nothing short of an utter.
In 207, the Romans eventually hunted him down at the "toe of Italy".
Where he was able to maintain a sort of guerrilla warfare yet and still literally.
Ironically, this very same patch of land later in Romanized his-story.
Would be introduced to mass slavery, in the second part of the century.
Meanwhile, the Romans had conquered Iberia.
A task that was easier said than done, but now set a whole new criteria.
Right after their success, two Roman generals were killed in battle.
At this time it seemed that almost all was lost, until a young Commander had taken up saddle.
Pubius Cornelius Scipio then took Carthaginia by surprise.
Proven worthy of his new position and was now on the rise.
Soon after, he had been sent to Sicily.
Then across the Mediterranean Sea.
But, before attacking Cartridge.
He, solidified an alliance with the Numidian King.
Left with no choice, the Carthaginian government's hands were forced.
They recalled Hannibal's still undefeated veterans in from Italy and home defense would be their new course.

Due to Rome's cockiness, the second Punic war would be fought in Alkebulan, instead of on Italian soil.
This is the very moment Hannibal's been living for his whole life, as his blood began to boil.
After several minor engagements, the two armies finally came head-to-head at Zama.
Every Roman Hannibal slayed by his sword, had been all in the name of his father.
Hannibal tried to repeat his encircling tactics, that had brought him victory 14 years earlier.
But, Scipio had better Calvary and his fighters were blood thirsty for murder.
Managing to escape, from the wrath of Rome.
The general now advised negotiations, from his Carthage home.
In the year 201, the two Nations had come to terms and agreements by signing a treaty.
Recognition of the Roman conquest in Iberia was one thing.
But, 50 annual installments of nothing less than ten thousand talents was way too greedy.
As for the great Hanniba'al Barca, he was forced to resign as general.
So, now he would focus on re-building the country's wealth, with only the bare minimum.
By 196, Cartridge's economy was now in ruins.
Full of pride.
The people of Carthage still chose to put, Hannibal's face on all of their coins.
Now, promoting democracy through the revenues, by way of its re-organization
Working on commerce trading, along with cultivation.
Hidden intentions among the court, were now on the rise.
Constitutional reformed members of aristocracy wanted Hannibal to die.
By informing the Roman senate, on his plans of treason.
Unknown, if the accusations were true.
But, before a Roman commission of inquiry was launched Hannibal ended up leaving.

He then fled on to Antioch, the capital of the Seleucid Empire.
In power for no more than a year and his house had been set afire.
At this time the Seleucid king and Rome both had similar interests.
The taking over of Macedonia and Greece were in both of their visions.
King Philip had eventually been defeated, in the second Macedonia war by Rome.
Following this event.
The Romans unexpectedly recalled all of their troops from Greece.
Leaving it unprotected and the Seleucid Empire attempting to fill that void.
Of course Hannibal was the commander, of this expeditionary force.
He advised the king to invade Italy, at this time of the Syrian war.
Due, to the Seleucid's arrogance and secret abhor.
The Carthaginian general was instead only given a minor naval role in which he was defeated in 190, by Rome's Maritime ally the Rhodes and ended up shipwrecked at shore.
Now that Rome had inflicted plenty of devastation and defeat.
Magnesia is where they had destroyed, their targeted enemy.
This left the king of the Seleucid's having to except, what is now called Turkey.
Then one of their governors had become independent and proclaimed himself to be greater Armenia King worthy.
At this time Hannibal's life was still in danger.
Where he remained at the Syrian Court, staying with the New king as he felt in favor.
In this newly established Royal Court, the nobility had followed Hannibal's advice and built a new capital.
Just South of modern-day Yerevan, is where they're building plan's had went graphical.
Later, the time had come for general Hannibal to flee once again.
Finding refuge at the court of King Prussia's of Bithynia and found himself back in command.
In 148, as an admiral the Carthaginian celebrated his last victory.
Defeating a Pergamene fleet, unknowingly this would be his last "W" in history.
The Romans intervened on behalf of the Paragon's favor.

This had been viewed as an act of war from the God's and the Romans were now their savor's.
In order to avoid capture and extradition.
The great general poisoned himself, on the coldest winter ever.
Dying all alone, with no one to bear witness. (183/182)

Stone Heads

Sculpted mega stone heads, with broad noses and cornrows built on shrine's.
Works of art from Mexico's, first known civilization in time.
Erected 14 ft high and shaped 7 feet wide.
Purely, in the image of only royal blood lines.
The sun God's people trade activities and influence has spread all throughout this region.
From South Central Mexico, all the way down to modern-day Nicaragua even.
Organized religion, cave rituals, ball courts, practices of sacrifice and the worship of animal God's.
Try telling a modern-day Mexican, that they were Black and surely they'll say it was all a façade.
Pale face beings tried so hard to destroy the evidence of our culture's existence.
But, what's so deeply rooted is always going to show up with consistence.
Living off the coast was good fishing for sea life including shrimps, turtles and clams.
Local supplies of plant foods, Palm nuts and fields full of agriculture were all throughout their lands.
Trading goods of Jade, serpentine, pottery, feathers, obsidian, Mica and rubber.
Connected to God's in the sky, while living in bodies on Earth and very familiar with Argatha down under.
As he stood on top of the mega pyramid structure of the Moon.
The priest-king overlooked thousands, as they cheered enjoying cups of chocolate as the rituals loomed.
Looking down the "Avenue of the dead", as another priest stood atop "The Sun Pyramid" to the left.
Wearing an outfit stitch together made up of pale skinned, blonde hair, seafarers in regards to his chef.

The priest-king then read from a calendar, dating back three thousand years before Christ.
Written in a West African Mende script, in connection with "Shango The Thunder God" and children were then religiously sacrificed.
Hieroglyphs were carved into walls to mark history in the making, of such things as iron ore made into mirrors.
The Olmecs inhabited and ruled the steamy gulf Coast lands for 800 years.
Many of their technologies and cultural traits were very important contributions to the America's.
Especially, being the pioneers of pyramid building, in Meso and South America.
Meso American trade before the Olmec's, only consisted of developing complex societies.
In which it was common for neighboring tribes and clans to trade on short-distance routes.
While lacking a universally accepted currency.
On arrival commerce and trading routes were developed with the Washitaw Nation of Louisiana, Black Californians, Jamassee, Califunami and other pre-Columbian Blacks in America.
Whom were all a part of a prehistoric worldwide trading Network that was developed over 100,000 years ago in Alkebulan.
Reigning supreme in their new lands as kings and queens.
Connected, civilized, cultured and clean.
Father's offered their daughters and some even their wives.
Many natives wanted to become one, with the sun God's peoples and bear new life.
African seeds were imported for crops, as well as animals, to create new species.
Around the same time that Asiatic American Indians, were still living in teepees.
Pyramids were being built fully equipped, with sewage lines to rid of feces.
Drawings of extraterrestrials, flying around in Craft's.
But, most notably in every depiction of Quat-Za-Cualto, he's always Black.

King of Songhai

Once a small kingdom along the Niger River.
Techniques of warfare made the empire of Songhai prominent figures.
Under attack by nomadic desert berbers.
Leaders of the now crumbling Mali empire, asked of the helping hands there nearby Songhai Brother's.
But, as the Malian empire began to disintegrate.
Rulers of Songhai took up the opportunity to penetrate.
Absorbing vast areas of a once-powerful rival.
Keeping wars going at the borders, became more than just acts of survival.
Only four years into his rule, Sunni Ali captured and fortify Timbuktu.
7 years later, they expanded into Djenne.
But, decisions were made by the king.
For its capital city of Goa, to remain the center of everything.
Now, under his control were three of the greatest trading cities along the Niger.
They were known as The Almighty Songhai empire.
Trade of gold, Kola and slaves.
From the south caravans of salt and copper had come.
Goods were also imported, from the Mediterranean Coast.
And guarding the river banks was a navy base of more than 400 boats.
This region was perfect for the breed of horses.
In which he commanded an elite Calvary to further rid of enemy forces.
In the river and on the lands.
He repulsed several attacks by the Mossi, whom resided south of his land.
Although Sunni Ali divided his territories, placed under the rule of his most trusted lieutenants.
As he returned from a conquest against the Fulani.
Plots were hatched against him, by one of his most closest lieutenants.
Poisoned by Muhammed Ture, his own sister son.

Whom also a year later, went to war with Sunni Baru.
Before taking over and founding a new dynasty of Songhai rulers under the sun.
Now, the new king of Songhai was "Askia the Great".
Askia Muhammad strengthen his empire, by making the largest in West African history up to this date.
Rapidly expanding, by trading goods with Europe and Asia.
The creation of many schools and consolidation of Islamic nations.
Also, a system of tribute-policing-trade routes and organized tax.
But, maybe he'd built too much power, for just one man.
Because his son Askia Musa thought he was getting soft and overthrew him behind his back.

About The Author

Clinzell "Boss Spade" Washington III was born during the dope era in the city of South Central, Los Angeles. Growing up in a time where drug and gang violence was at an all-time high on a national scale, Boss Spade joined the East Coast Crips at 11 years old and later served his first juvenile camp sentence of 18 months for robbery in the Violent Alternative Program of Challengers Camp Smith. This would only be the beginning of a life of crime-filled activities.

Ultimately spending half of his life in and out of juvenile halls, camps, CYA, CDCR, Wackenhut, and CCA facilities across California and America, he was last released in June 2018, after doing 4 years off of a 12-year sentence. Being granted an early release date because of prison overcrowding. The Non-Violent Second Strikers law was voted into California's penal system through Proposition 57.

Since his release, the author has obtained the license of a certified Pest Control Technician. But sadly, his license was revoked by the California Structural Pest Control Board because of his criminal past. Not letting anything stop him, he completed his book that he started writing while in prison. He started his own publishing company. He was discharged from parole two years after his release with no violations.

Clinzell launched his own branded real Italian leather shoe line https://www.aliveshoes.com/lacoastanostra-4 and https://www.aliveshoes.com/lacoastanostra-8 and recently graduated with a degree in business. This is the author's first book, and it was written in the efforts of giving the reader real, true, raw, authentic feelings and *Thoughts of A Convicted Felon: Live From The L.A. County Jail.*

www.ingramcontent.com/pod-product-compliance
Lightning Source LLC
Chambersburg PA
CBHW030905080526
44589CB00010B/159